Autism

Autism
an introduction to psychological theory

Francesca Happé

Harvard University Press
Cambridge, Massachusetts
1995

First published in 1994 by UCL Press Limited
The name of University College London (UCL) is a registered trade mark
used by UCL Press with the consent of the owner.

Library of Congress Catalog number 94-77278

ISBN 0-674-05312-5

Contents

Preface

This book is intended as an introduction to current thinking about autism. There are many excellent practical guides to autism for parents and teachers (Wing 1971, Howlin & Rutter 1987, Aarons & Gittens 1991, Baron-Cohen & Bolton 1993). Wonderful and evocative books have been written by the parents of children with autism, which give insight into the everyday life and personal development of the individual (e.g. Park 1987, Hart 1989, McDonnell 1993). Increasingly, able individuals with autism are telling their own stories, a testament to their courage and talents (e.g. Grandin 1984, Grandin & Scariano 1986, Miedzianik 1986, Williams 1992). For those with an interest in theoretical and research issues, there are books which put forward a single author's theory of the condition (e.g. Frith 1989a, Hobson 1993a). There are also weighty collections of chapters by experts, each writing in detail about a particular facet of the disorder (Schopler & Mesibov 1983, 1985, 1987, Cohen et al. 1987, Dawson 1989, Baron-Cohen et al. 1993b).

This book aims to serve a function not intended by any of these books: to give a concise and readable introduction to current research and theory in the field of autism. As far as possible I have tried to give a balanced overview of the field. However, I have also attempted to synthesize and critically assess work in the area – which necessarily introduces my own perspective. I hope that this will encourage readers to think critically and formulate their own research questions and hypotheses.

Although this book is not a practical guide to the care and education of people with autism, I hope that it may be of interest to parents and teachers, who are in many senses the true experts. The primary intended audience, however, is undergraduate and postgraduate students of psychology or related subjects, who – like me – find themselves captivated and mesmerized by the enigma of autism.

FRANCESCA HAPPÉ

MRC Cognitive Development Unit

Acknowledgements

I should like to thank the children and adults with autism, and their parents and teachers, who have taught me so much, and shown me how much more I have yet to learn.

All my colleagues at the CDU have helped, directly or indirectly. In particular, I have been lucky to have the opportunity to learn from John Morton, Alan Leslie and Annette Karmiloff-Smith. It is to Uta Frith, however, that the biggest thanks must go: she has been an incomparable tutor and mentor, as well as giving invaluable encouragement and support. I could not have had a better supervisor, colleague or friend in my explorations of autism.

Neil O'Connor and Beate Hermelin gave me my first opportunity to meet people with autism, when I was still an undergraduate. Other colleagues should also be thanked, for their intellectual generosity and practical advice; Simon Baron-Cohen, Dermot Bowler, Chris Frith, Peter Hobson, Jim Russell and Marian Sigman. Friends have also helped me to write this book, by discussing ideas, and putting up with my sometimes autistically-narrow interest in this area; Daniel, Liz, Fran, James and Caroline.

Some of the material in this book first appeared in the course handbook for the University of Birmingham's distance learning course on autism. I am grateful to Tina Tilstone and the members of the course's steering committee for their help and advice.

Finally, I would like to thank my family for never failing to give support, enthusiasm and encouragement. A. M. D. G.

Chapter 1
Introduction

The aim of this book is to acquaint you with current research and thinking about autism, in a concise and comprehensive way. Clearly it cannot be exhaustive in this respect – or it would become like so many "handbooks" which are so large they need two hands to lift! Further reading is suggested in two ways – references in the text will allow you to find out more about specific issues raised, while suggested reading (usually in the form of books or review articles) appears at the end of each chapter, allowing you to deepen your knowledge of those aspects of autism which particularly interest you. Throughout the book the discussion of points has been kept as brief as possible, in the hope that the book will provide a manageable overview of autism, tying together a number of quite different areas. It should whet your appetite for the more detailed consideration of aspects of autism, provided by the suggested readings.

Explaining autism: levels of explanation

If a Martian asked you what an apple is, you might reply that it is a fruit, or that it is something you eat, you might describe it as roundish and red, or you might try to give its composition in terms of vitamins, water, sugars, and so on. The way you answer the question will probably depend on why you think the Martian wants to know – is he hungry, does he want to be able to recognize an apple, or is he simply curious?

Similarly, different types of answer can be given to the question "What is autism?" None of these answers is *the* answer, since each answer is appropriate for a different sense of the question. In order to find the right answer for the question in any one context, we need to think about our reasons for asking. One can think about this distinction between the different senses of a question in terms of different *levels of explanation*.

In the study of autism, three levels in particular are useful; the biological, the cognitive, and the behavioural. It is important to keep these levels distinct, because each of the three levels does a different job in our understanding of autism. So, for example, to inform the search for a cure for a disorder, it may be appropriate to look at the biological nature of the problem, while to inform management it may be more important to consider the behavioural description of the problem.

Morton & Frith (1994) have introduced a specific diagrammatic tool for thinking about levels of explanation in developmental disorders such as autism. Figure 1.1, taken from Morton & Frith (1994), shows their causal models of the three levels and the possible relations between these levels, in different types of disorder. Pattern (a) is the case of a disorder defined by its unitary biological origin (O), which may have diverse effects at the cognitive and behavioural levels. An example of this type of disorder might be fragile X syndrome, as currently conceptualized; individuals are said to have fragile X syndrome on the basis of chromosomal analysis of their genetic material. However, not all individuals so defined have the same cognitive or behavioural features: while many will have severe learning difficulties (mental handicap) and show gaze avoidance, others may have normal intelligence and appear socially well adjusted. Pattern (b) shows a disorder with multiple biological causes, and several different behavioural manifestations, but a single defining cognitive deficit (∅). Autism may be one such disorder (see Ch. 5). Dyslexia, according to some cognitive theories (also modelled by Morton & Frith 1994, e.g. Snowling 1987), may be another example; a number of biological causes may converge in causing a cognitive deficit in the phonological system, leading in turn to multiple behavioural manifestations (e.g. slow reading, poor spelling, poor auditory

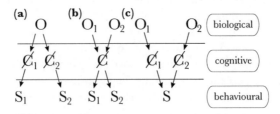

Figure 1.1   Morton & Frith's (1994) causal models of three types of disorder (by kind permission of the authors).

memory, poor rhyme and sound-segmentation skills). Pattern (c) is the case of a disorder defined by its behavioural features (symptoms, S) alone, with multiple biological causes and cognitive natures. Attention deficit disorder, as currently diagnosed, may be such a disorder; children who show extreme distractibility, for whatever reason, may be grouped together under this label for the purposes of treatment and management.

Throughout this book, I will be using the notion of levels of explanation, to keep separate different issues and questions. In Chapter 3, the diagnosis of autism is discussed, and the focus is on the behavioural level − since autism is currently recognized on the basis of behavioural features rather than, for example, biological aetiology. In Chapter 4, the biological level is addressed, since evidence is now overwhelmingly in favour of a biological cause for autism. In Chapters 5 and 6 the remaining of the three levels is discussed − the cognitive level. Cognitive theories aim to span the gulf between biology and behaviour − between the brain and action − through hypotheses about the mind. This level − the level of cognition − is the primary focus for this book. The term "cognitive" as used here is not to be contrasted with affective. Rather, it is intended to cover all aspects of the working of the mind, including thoughts and feelings. This level of analysis might also be called the "psychological" level, except that psychology also includes the study of behaviour.

Keeping the three levels of explanation (biology, cognition, behaviour) distinct helps in thinking about a number of issues to do with autism. So, for example, people often ask whether autism is part of the normal continuum of social behaviour − are we all "a bit autistic"? The answer to this question is different at the different levels of explanation. At the behavioural level the answer may be "yes" − at least in some respects: the person with autism may *behave* much like the very shy normal person in some situations, and everyone shows some stereotypies (e.g. finger-tapping). However, at the biological level people with autism are almost certainly different from people who do not suffer from autism − something in the anatomy or neurophysiology of their brains is responsible for their handicap, and is not present in "normal" people. At the cognitive level too (according to the theory you hold), people with autism may be quite distinct, and not simply at one end of a normal continuum. So, for example, very different *reasons* may underlie apparently similar behaviour by the individual with autism and by the "normal" person − think of a person with autism and a "normal" rebellious teenager, both of whom may dress inappropriately for social situations. So, the autistic child's social difficulties probably have a quite different cause (at the cognitive level) from the "normal" shy person's – although the behaviours produced (avoiding large groups, social anxiety, inappropriate social behaviour such as odd eye contact) may be very similar.

Questions about the borderlands of autism are particularly relevant when one considers the most high-functioning people with autism. Chapter 7 discusses current research looking at this group, while Chapter 8 introduces the new and increasingly influential diagnosis of "Asperger's syndrome", which may be seen as a response to the recent focus on the more able end of the autistic continuum. Chapter 9 considers the borderlands of autism through a discussion of differential diagnosis, and the practical issue of assessing therapies and "cures". Lastly, Chapter 10 re-examines the question, "Is autism part of the 'normal' continuum?", and looks again at some of the special skills, as well as deficits, which people with autism exhibit.

Explaining autism: timescales of explanation

As well as trying to answer the question "What is autism?", this book explores why or how autism occurs. In other words, it is concerned with *causal* theories of autism. In thinking about causal explanations it is useful to keep distinct not only three *levels* of description but also three *timescales*. Causes can be examined in terms of *evolutionary* time, taking as the unit for discussion the gene, and considering pressures acting in the process of natural selection. A second timescale of cause is *development*, where the individual (or the biological, behavioural or cognitive mechanism within the individual) is considered. Developmental time includes key features like the existence of critical periods in some systems, where a finite window of time exists for specific causes to have specific effects (e.g. imprinting in the chick) – the same causal agent acting on the organism after this time will not have the same consequences. Lastly, there is the time span of on-line mechanisms, the moment-to-moment or *processing* time.

In considering autism the latter two timescales are particularly important (see, for example, Ch. 6). Two examples may help to clarify the distinction, and to illustrate that the same deficit may have rather different effects in terms of disruptions to development and disruptions to processing.

Think of the effects of large quantities of alcohol acting as a cause on the three timescales. In evolutionary time, imagine that the existence of alcohol in foodstuffs leads to the selection of individuals with the ability to taste this substance and avoid consuming large quantities of foods containing alcohol – since being drunk does not increase reproductive success! In developmental time, alcohol has different effects – in large quantities it may hamper the physical and mental development of the fetus. Still in developmental terms, intake of large quantities of alcohol may have long-term effects on adults, for example cirrhosis of the liver. In terms of processing time, however, the effects of alcohol are usually pleasant – that's why we drink it! In large amounts, however, it has effects on processing, for example causing slurring of speech and loss of balance. These are "on-line" effects in the sense that they persist only for so long as the maintaining cause is there – the high blood alcohol level. The developmental effects, however, may persist, even after the individual has sobered up.

Another illustration of the three levels might be the effect of lack of calcium on bone formation. It is currently believed that the level of calcium intake (amongst other factors) affects the strength of bones. However, this statement is true only at the developmental level. Women who drink a lot of milk in their twenties may be less likely to develop brittle bones in their sixties and seventies. However, drinking a glass of milk today will not stop you breaking your leg tomorrow! Calcium does not work on-line to strengthen bones, and there is no instant effect. Similarly, as long as you drank lots of milk as a young woman, you can give the stuff up in your seventies – you are no longer building your bones (the developmental work of calcium is over). In terms of evolutionary time, interestingly, osteoporosis affecting postmenopausal women would probably have no causal effect – natural selection would not act to favour women who have strong bones after childbearing age since this would probably have no advantage in terms of reproductive success.

These examples may seem a long way from autism but, as will emerge in Chapter 6, psychological theories of autism can easily confuse developmental and processing causes.

Some facts and fiction

While the question "What is autism?" can be answered at a number of levels – as will be explored further in Chapters 3, 4, 5 and 6 – there are some statements which can be made concerning what autism is *not*. It may be useful at this early stage to clear away some of the myths and misunderstandings about autism.

Autism is *not* caused by "refrigerator parenting".

Autism *is* a biologically based disorder.

Autism is *not* confined to childhood.

Autism *is* a developmental disorder which lasts throughout life.

Autism is *not* always characterized by special, or "savant", skills.

Autism *is* found at all IQ levels, but is commonly accompanied by general learning difficulties (mental handicap).

Autism is *not* just a "shell" within which a "normal" child is waiting to get out.

Autism *is* a severe disorder of communication, socialization and imagination.

Chapter 2

The history of autism

"He wandered about smiling, making stereotyped movements with his fingers, crossing them about in the air. He shook his head from side to side, whispering or humming the same three-note tune. He spun with great pleasure anything he could seize upon to spin . . . When taken into a room, he completely disregarded the people and instantly went for objects, preferably those that could be spun . . . He angrily shoved away the hand that was in his way or the foot that stepped on one of his blocks . . . "   (Kanner 1943; reprinted in Kanner 1973: 3–5)

This description, of a five-year-old boy called Donald, was written over 50 years ago. Kanner saw Donald and made these observations in 1938, and they appear in his landmark paper "Autistic disturbances of affective contact", published in 1943. Clinicians and teachers today remark on similar features. Autism itself, then, has changed little over the half century since its recognition. But what about the years before 1943? Is autism a new disorder? Probably not. Uta Frith (1989a) has speculated that we can find evidence of autism throughout history. She mentions the "Blessed Fools" of Old Russia, who were revered for their unworldliness. The apparent insensitivity to pain, bizarre behaviour, innocence, and lack of social awareness that these "Blessed Fools" showed, suggest that they may have had autism.

Almost certainly, autism has always existed. Folktales can be found in almost every culture which tell stories of naive or "simple" individuals with odd behaviour and a striking lack of common sense. The following folktales come from two very different cultures, but each centres on naive and over-literal understanding of communication – a very characteristic feature of high-functioning individuals with autism (see Chs 3 and 5). The first tale comes from India:

> One time Sheikh Chilli was hotly in love with a girl, and he said to his mother: "What is the best way of making a girl fond of one?" Said his mother: "The best plan is to sit by the well, and when she comes to draw water, just throw a pebble at her and smile."
>
> The Sheikh went to the well, and when the girl appeared, he flung a big stone at her and broke her head. All the people turned out and were going to murder him, but when he explained matters, they agreed that he was the biggest fool in the world.
>
> (From *Folktales of India*, Kang & Kang 1988)

The second folktale comes from Malta:

> In a village there lived a boy called Gahan. It was Sunday and Gahan's mother wanted to go to church early. But Gahan didn't like getting up in the mornings, so he said he would stay in bed. When his mother was ready to go, she came into Gahan's room.
>
> "I'm off to church now," she said. "When you get up, if you decide to come to the church, be sure and pull the door behind you."
>
> "Don't worry, mother," said Gahan, "I won't forget."
>
> After a while Gahan climbed out of bed, washed and dressed and was just about to leave when he remembered what his mother had said. He opened the front door, pulled it down, held it by the knocker and began to pull it along behind him.
>
> . . . You can imagine how all the people laughed when they saw Gahan walking along the street dragging the door behind him. When he arrived at the church he walked straight in. But he made such a banging and clattering noise that everyone turned to see what was happening. They, too, thought that it was very funny, but Gahan's poor mother was very embarrassed.
>
> "What on earth are you doing?" she asked.
>
> "Well, mother," answered Gahan, "you asked me to pull the door behind me if I left the house, didn't you?"
>
> (From *Folktales from Australia's children of the world*, Smith 1979)

These tales suggest that the odd behaviour and naivety of the person with autism have been recognized in many different cultures. It is interesting that the subjects of this sort of folktale are almost always male; autism is more than twice as common among men as among women (see Ch. 4).

Why did it take so long for autism to receive a name? Perhaps because autism is so rare (see Ch. 4). Perhaps because it is often accompanied by general learning difficulties, which have themselves become better understood in this century. Although clinicians before Kanner had described children who we would now diagnose as suffering from autism, it was not until Kanner wrote about a group of 11 children with a puzzling but similar constellation of symptoms, that the syndrome of autism was really recognized. What was "autism" for Kanner?

Leo Kanner's autism

Kanner's first paper on autism highlights a set of features he perceived to be characteristic of all the children he saw. These features included the following:

"*Extreme autistic aloneness*" – the children failed to relate to people normally, and appeared to be happiest when left alone. This lack of social responsiveness appeared to Kanner to start very early in life, as shown by the autistic infant's failure to put out his arms to the parent who was about to pick him up, or to mould himself to the parent's body when held.

"*Anxiously obsessive desire for the preservation of sameness*" – the children were extremely upset by changes of routine or surroundings. A different route to school, a rearrangement of furniture, would cause a tantrum, and the child could not be calmed until the familiar order was restored.

"*Excellent rote memory*" – the children Kanner saw showed an ability to memorize large amounts of effectively meaningless material (e.g. an encyclopaedia index page), which was out of line with their apparent severe learning difficulties or mental handicap in other respects.

"*Delayed echolalia*" – the children repeated language they heard, but failed to use words to communicate beyond their immediate needs. The echolalia probably explains the reversal of pronouns which Kanner remarked upon – that the children would use "you" when referring to themselves and "I" for the other person. This usage would follow from a direct repetition of the other speaker's remark. In the same way, children with autism commonly use the whole of a question as a request for the item which usually follows (e.g. "Do you want a sweet?" meaning "I want a sweet").

"*Oversensitivity to stimuli*" – Kanner noticed that many of the children he saw reacted strongly to certain noises and to objects such as vacuum cleaners, elevators and even the wind. Some also showed feeding problems or food fads.

"*Limitation in the variety of spontaneous activity*" – shown in the children's repetitious movements, verbalizations and interests. However, Kanner felt that the children showed a good relation to objects, often showing surprising dexterity in spinning things or completing jigsaw puzzles.

"*Good cognitive potentialities*" – Kanner believed that the outstanding memory and dexterity shown by some of his cases reflected a superior intelligence, despite the fact that many of the children had been considered to have severe learning difficulties. This strong impression of intelligence – that a child with autism *could* if only they *would* – is often felt by parents and teachers. The good memory in particular is tantalizing – leading one to feel that if only it could be turned to some practical use, the child might learn well. An impression of intelligence is also given by the lack of any physical stigmata in most cases of autism. Unlike children with many types of severe learning difficulties (e.g. Down's syndrome), children with autism usually look "normal". Kanner remarked on the "intelligent physiognomies" of his cases, and other authors have described children with autism as unusually beautiful.

"*Highly intelligent families*" – Kanner remarked that all his cases had intellectual parents. However, this is probably due simply to a referral bias – Kanner's sample is unlikely to have been representative. Kanner also described the parents as cold, although in his first paper he was very far from a psychogenic theory. Instead he states, "these children have come into the world with innate inability to form the usual, biologically provided affective contact with people".

In his later writing (Kanner & Eisenberg 1956) Kanner isolated just two of these many features as the key elements of autism: "extreme isolation and the obsessive insistence on the preservation of sameness". The other symptoms he considered to be either secondary to and caused by these two elements (e.g. communicative impairments), or non-specific to autism (e.g. stereotypies). In Chapter 3, Kanner's description of autism will be reassessed, and the issue of universality and specificity of symptoms will be discussed. Current diagnostic criteria will also be examined.

Hans Asperger

The history of autism is something like waiting for a bus – nothing for years and then two come along together! In 1944, just one year after Kanner published his influential paper, an Austrian physician, Hans Asperger, published a dissertation concerning "autistic psychopathy" in childhood. It has taken nearly 50 years for Asperger's original paper, "Die 'Autistischen Psychopathen' im Kindesalter", to appear in translation in English (Frith 1991b). Hans Asperger deserves credit for some very striking insights into autism: some insights which Kanner (1943) lacked and which it has taken us many years of research to rediscover. Before considering these particular observations of Asperger's, it is worth noting the many features on which the two physicians agreed.

Kanner's and Asperger's descriptions are surprisingly similar in many ways, especially when one remembers that each was unaware of the other's ground-breaking paper. Their choice of the term "autistic" to label their patients is itself a striking coincidence. This choice reflects their common belief that the child's social problems were the most important and characteristic feature of the disorder. The term "autistic" comes from Bleuler (1908), who used the word (from the Greek "autos" meaning "self") to describe the social withdrawal seen in adults with schizophrenia. Both Kanner and Asperger believed the social handicap in autism to be innate (in Kanner's words) or constitutional (as Asperger put it), and to persist through life into adulthood. In addition, Kanner and Asperger both noted the children's poor eye contact, their stereotypies of word and movement, and their marked resistance to change. The two authors report the common finding of isolated special interests, often in bizarre and idiosyncratic objects or topics. Both seem to have been struck by the attractive appearance of the children they saw. Kanner and Asperger make a point of distinguishing the disorder they describe from schizophrenia, on the basis of three features: the improvement rather than deterioration in their patients, the absence of hallucinations, and the fact that these children appeared to be abnormal from their earliest years, rather than showing a decline in ability after initially good functioning. Lastly, both Kanner and Asperger believed that they had observed similar traits – of social withdrawal or incompetence, obsessive delight in routine, and the pursuit of special interests to the exclusion of all else – in the parents of many of their patients.

There are three main areas in which Asperger's and Kanner's reports disagree, if we believe that they were describing the same sort of child. The first and most striking of these is the child's *language abilities*. Kanner reported that three of his 11 patients never spoke at all, and that the other children did not use what language they had to communicate: "As far as the communicative functions of speech are concerned, there is no fundamental dif-

11

ference between the eight speaking and the three mute children" (Kanner 1943). While phonology (as demonstrated in accurate echolalia) and vocabulary were often excellent, Kanner concluded that of his 11 cases "In none . . . has language . . . served to convey meaning". The picture in all is of a child with profound communicative difficulties and delay; in seven of the 11 cases so profound that deafness was initially suspected (but ruled out). Asperger, by contrast, reported that each of his four case study patients (and, by implication, most of the unspecified number of such children he treated) spoke fluently. Although two of his patients showed some delay, this was followed in both cases by a rapid mastery of language, and it is difficult to imagine any of his cases having been mistaken for deaf. All four cases, by the age of examination (between 6 and 9 years old), spoke "like little adults". Asperger notes their "freedom" and "originality" in language use, and reports that two of his four cases had a tendency to tell "fantastic stories".

Asperger's description also conflicts with Kanner's on the subject of *motor abilities* and co-ordination. Kanner (1943) reported clumsiness in only one case, and remarks on the dexterity of four of his patients. He concluded that "several of the children were somewhat clumsy in gait and gross motor performance, but all were very skilful in terms of finer muscle coordination" – in line with their success on the Seguin form board (in which dexterity plays a part) and their ability to spin objects. Asperger, by contrast, described all four of his patients as clumsy, and recounted their problems not only with school sports (gross co-ordination), but also with fine motor skills such as writing. This feature is part of a larger contrast in Asperger's and Kanner's beliefs. Kanner believed the autistic child to have a specific impairment in social understanding, with better relations to objects than to people: while his children showed "excellent, purposeful and 'intelligent' relations to objects" their "relations to people [were] altogether different". Asperger, on the other hand, believed that his patients showed disturbances in both areas: "the essential abnormality in autism is a disturbance of the lively relationship with the whole environment" (Asperger 1944, translated in Frith 1991b).

The last area of disagreement in the clinical pictures painted by Asperger and Kanner is that of the child's *learning abilities*. Kanner believed that his patients were best at learning rote fashion, but Asperger felt that his patients performed "best when the child can produce spontaneously", and suggests that they are "abstract thinkers".

How are we to understand and resolve these contradictions? One possibility would be simply to discount Asperger's insights in these three areas, and retain Kanner's opinions, which are by now "tried and tested" and found to be true of great numbers of autistic children. That we have confirmation of Kanner's clinical description should come as no surprise, after all it is his descriptions primarily that have outlined what we call autism. As is becoming increasingly obvious, however, many children and adults in need of care are neglected by clinicians who's definition of autism is based on a narrow stereotype of Kanner's cases. As Wing & Gould (1979) pointed out, the autistic person's problems may manifest themselves differently according to age and ability, meaning that there is a spectrum of behaviours that arise from similar underlying handicaps (see Ch. 3). If we hold rigidly to Kanner's descriptions we are in danger of neglecting, for example, the autistic person who no longer avoids social interaction, but instead seeks it in inappropriate ways.

If we decide, then, to retain Asperger's insights, we have to decide whether he is describing a different sort of child, or the same sort of child from a different viewpoint or at a different age. On the subject of learning, for example, one might argue that *both* Kanner and Asperger are correct, and that the same autistic child may indeed benefit greatly from learning things rote fashion using his apparently excellent memory for unconnected facts (and given the child's often limited insight into the underlying principles) where teaching is involved, but be in general better at picking up knowledge when following his own interests than when being taught. It is hard, however, to reach such compromises when one turns to Asperger and Kanner's positions on language and motor skills. These areas, then, become – not surprisingly – the key issues for those who feel that Asperger was describing a different group of children from Kanner. The debate concerning Asperger's syndrome, and its relation to "Kanner-type" autism is taken up in Chapter 8.

Conclusions

Autism, then, is a relatively new diagnosis, although the disorder itself has probably always existed. A great deal has been learnt about the syndrome since it first received a name. While there is often debate as to the value or danger of labelling children and adults as having a specific disorder, it seems unlikely that so much progress would have been made over the last 50 years, had not Kanner and Asperger put a name to features which seemed to characterize a group of very special children.

Much has been learnt about autism, but much still remains to be understood. In the next chapters, the current state of knowledge concerning the behavioural, biological and cognitive nature of autism will be reviewed, and some continuing puzzles and future research questions discussed.

Suggested reading

Frith, U. 1989a. *Autism: explaining the enigma*, chs 2 & 3. Oxford: Basil Blackwell.

Kanner, L. & L. Eisenberg 1956. Early infantile autism 1943–1955. *American Journal of Orthopsychiatry 26*, 55–65.

Wing, L. 1991. The relationship between Asperger's syndrome and Kanner's autism. In *Autism and Asperger syndrome*, U. Frith (ed.), 93–121. Cambridge: Cambridge University Press.

Chapter 3

Autism at the behavioural level

Chapter 2 discussed how autism was first described and named by Leo Kanner in 1943 and Hans Asperger in 1944. Then, as now, autism was defined on the basis of behaviour. For Kanner, the essential and defining symptoms of autism were the child's "autistic aloneness" and "obsessive desire for the preservation of sameness" (Kanner & Eisenberg 1956). Although Kanner's early descriptions are very evocative, and many of the children with autism seen today conform exactly to the picture he drew, the diagnosis of autism has changed in a number of ways as more has been learnt about the disorder.

Necessary and sufficient features

When we ask what the defining features of a disorder are, we are asking something about the symptoms that are necessary and sufficient for the diagnosis to be made. Any disorder will have core features which a person must show to receive the diagnosis. But there will also be non-necessary features that a patient may or may not show. The core features alone will be sufficient for the diagnosis, and will distinguish the disorder from other conditions.

Since Kanner's initial insight was based on a limited number of cases referred to his clinic, his description naturally included some features that are secondary to, or even unrelated to, autism (e.g. social class bias). The starting point for progress in discovering the nature and cause of autism was built in turn on a wealth of epidemiological and clinical data which has allowed the stripping away of those symptoms which, while being shown *by* some children with autism, are not symptoms *of* autism itself. Without such a "cleaning up" process, attempts at explanation would be unlikely to succeed, since researchers would stand a good chance of spending time trying to explain features that are in fact neither universal nor specific to autism. In the past, effort has sadly been wasted in just this way, and such non-necessary features have sometimes been suggested as causes of autism. An example is the "stimulus overselectivity hypothesis" of Lovaas et al. (1971), which suggested that the handicaps in autism are caused by over-focused attention. This promising theory floundered when research showed that a failure to pay attention to multiple aspects of the environment is associated with severe learning difficulties (mental handicap) in general and is not specific to autism.

Reviews of the epidemiological work conclude that, of the host of symptoms shown by people with autism, many are not specific to autism. So, for example, Wing & Wing (1971) found that while more than 80 per cent of children with autism in their sample showed a preference for the proximal senses (smell, taste, touch), this preference was also seen in 87 per cent of partially blind and deaf children, 47 per cent of subjects with Down's syndrome and 28 per cent of normal children. Since features such as language problems, stereotypies and mental retardation can be found in other, non-autistic, children they cannot be primary and sufficient causes of the autistic child's other problems. In order to focus on features special and specific to autism, studies typically contrast subjects with autism with control groups made up of children or adults with the same level of general learning difficulties (or mental handicap) who do not have autism. By matching groups for IQ or developmental level (mental age, MA), one can be more confident that group differences are due to the subjects' autism and not merely a result of the mental handicap which accompanies autism in around three-quarters of all cases (see Ch. 4).

The spectrum in autism

Kanner's original description of autism has also been modified over time with the recognition that the same handicap may be manifest in a number of different ways. So, while some children with autism avoid social contact, like Kanner's cases, others are merely passive, or even actively sociable in a peculiar fashion (see Fig. 3.1) (Wing & Gould 1979). The clinical picture of autism has been found to vary across and even within individuals, according to intellectual ability and age. The picture that autism presents, then, varies greatly, and Wing (1988) introduced the concept of a *spectrum* of dis-

the aloof   the passive   the odd

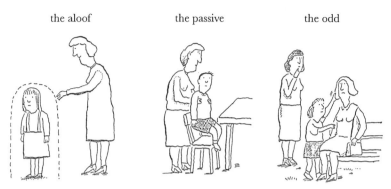

Figure 3.1   Three types of social impairment (by kind permission of the artist, Axel Scheffler). Reprinted from Frith 1989a.

orders in autism to capture this idea of a range of manifestations of the same handicap.

Is autism a true syndrome?

A major problem exists with diagnosis at the behavioural level: behavioural features may occur together merely by chance. Is it unjustified, then, to talk of autism as a syndrome (i.e. a pattern of symptoms that cluster together)? Should autism be seen, rather, as an unlucky assortment of handicaps with no common cause (just as one child might, by chance, be colour blind, tall, and red haired). The fundamental work in answering this question was done by Wing & Gould (1979), who conducted an epidemiological survey of all children living in the Camberwell area of south London. From the total population aged under 15 years (35,000), all children known to the social, educational or health services (914 in all) were screened. Children were selected from this group if they had severe learning difficulties, and/ or if they showed one of the following: social impairment, verbal and non-verbal language impairment, repetitive/stereotyped activities.

   The screening resulted in a group of 132 children, all of whom attended special schools, and who ranged in age from 2 to 18 years (at the time of assessment). The children were observed and given medical and psychological tests, and their carers were interviewed with the Handicap, Behaviour and Skills Schedule (Wing & Gould 1978). The group was divided on the basis of social behaviour into 58 children with appropriate social interaction

17

(for their mental age) and 74 socially impaired subjects (of whom 17 had classic autism, by Kanner & Eisenberg's (1956) criteria of social aloofness and elaborate routines). The groups did not differ in age, but there were significantly more males in the socially impaired group than in the sociable group. In addition there were significant differences in communicative and play behaviours in the two groups: 90 per cent of the impaired group (versus only 50 per cent of the sociable subjects) were either mute or echolalic at the time of the interview, and 97 per cent of the impaired group (versus 24 per cent of the sociable group) showed no or only repetitive symbolic play. In the sociable group, all subjects showed symbolic play except those with a language comprehension age below 20 months – a mental age below which pretence would not be expected, since normal children only manifest this ability in the second year of life. By contrast, the socially impaired subjects with a language comprehension age over 20 months still showed communication deficits and poverty of symbolic play. Wing & Gould (1978: 25) concluded that "all the children with social impairments had repetitive stereotyped behaviour and almost all had absence or abnormalities of language and symbolic activities. Thus the study showed a marked tendency for these problems to occur together". The association between these three handicaps also emerged when the Camberwell sample was divided on the basis of types of play shown (Wing et al. 1977) rather than social functioning.

This association between deficits in socialization, communication and imagination was also found in a group of 761 adults in a mental handicap hospital (Shah et al. 1982). Abnormal speech was shown by 75 per cent of those with social impairment, versus 14 per cent of those showing social interaction appropriate for their mental age. Symbolic activity (including interest in books and films, concern for others, and mental age appropriate play) was lacking in 73 per cent of the socially impaired group, and only 8 per cent of the sociable group. It appears, then, that handicaps in social understanding, in communication, and in imagination tend to co-occur in the same individual, and do not simply arise together by chance in those individuals who are diagnosed as suffering from autism.

The triad of impairments

Problems of *socialization, communication* and *imagination* are sufficient and necessary to capture much of the behaviour found to be specific and universal to autism. A person with autism may have no speech or gesture whatsoever, they may be echolalic only, or they may have fluent but oddly used language; but all these variations can be seen as manifestations of a communication handicap. The toddler with autism may spin the wheels of a toy car instead of pretending to park or clean it, while the adult with autism may show no interest in fiction in the form of TV soaps or novels, preferring to read telephone directories; both of these pictures reflect an underlying impairment in imagination. Similarly, the person with autism may run away from social approaches, may seem cut off and passive, or may pester people with questions and monologues; but these behaviours all demonstrate a fundamental lack of social understanding (Wing 1988).

As well as these core features, which all children and adults with autism show, there are many other characteristics which are typical but not universal to autism. These include striking discrepancies on intelligence test batteries, where non-verbal ability (on, for example, jigsaw-type tests) often far exceeds verbal skills (Lockyer & Rutter 1970). Around 1 in 10 people with autism show so-called savant abilities, much in advance of their overall IQ, in music, drawing or calculation (Rimland 1978, Rimland & Hill 1984). Many individuals with autism show motor stereotypies such as rocking, walking on tip-toes, hand-flapping, or flicking their fingers rapidly in front of their eyes. Self-stimulatory behaviours such as these, which occasionally involve self-injury through hand-biting or head-banging, can also be found in non-autistic people with severe mental handicap. More specific to autism is the "desire for the preservation of sameness" which Kanner noted, and which can range from wearing the same clothes every day, to the imposition of elaborate routines and arrangements of objects which must not be altered by family or teachers. In general, these non-social features of autism are little understood, but Chapter 10 discusses one preliminary theory which attempts to address these puzzling aspects of autism.

Diagnosis

The set of three core impairments, which has become known as Wing's triad, is the basis for the diagnosis of autism today (Rutter & Schopler 1987). Diagnosis of autism in both of the major diagnostic instruments currently used by clinicians (*Diagnostic and statistical manual of mental disorders*, third revised edn (DSM-III-R), American Psychiatric Association 1987, and *International classification of diseases*, 10th revision (ICD–10), World Health Organization 1990) is based on three fundamental impairments which

capture Wing's triad:
- qualitative impairment in reciprocal social interaction;
- qualitative impairment in verbal and nonverbal communication and in imaginative activity;
- markedly restricted repertoire of activities and interests.

The full diagnostic criteria for autism in DSM-III-R can be seen in Table 3.1.

The triad of impairments in socialization, communication and imagination forms the background for research into autism, for it defines the problem to be solved and the picture to be explained. A minimum requirement for psychological theories of autism, then, is to explain the co-occurrence of these three deficits (see Chs 5 and 6).

Early indicators of autism

At what age can autism be diagnosed? At present, a reliable diagnosis of autism is rare before the age of 3 or 4 years. This is primarily because the types of behaviours which are impaired in autism (according to the diagnostic criteria above) do not emerge reliably in normal children until this age. However, in recent years there has been increasing interest in the possibility of pinpointing earlier indicators of autism. The search for very early signs that would allow one to predict which children would turn out to have autism has been prompted by two rather different concerns. Practical considerations have pressed for earlier diagnosis in the hope that very early intervention might have a stronger remedial effect. However, it is far from clear, as yet, what form this intervention should take. Theoretical considerations urge the early identification of autism in order to explore the nature of the primary deficit, and the causal directions in development (see Ch. 6) – for example, do deficits in imitation lead to or result from difficulties in social interaction? While many researchers, including Kanner and Asperger, have considered autism to be present from birth, this does not, of course, mean that there will necessarily be *signs* of autism from birth. Many aspects of the innate constitution of a child are not evident in the infant, and take time to mature and develop (e.g. innately "programmed" hormonal changes at puberty).

Early indicator studies are of two major types; retrospective and prospective. *Retrospective studies* work backwards, taking a population and looking at their developmental history. Such studies are open to the criticism that remembering may be influenced by subsequent outcome – remembering with the benefit of hindsight may be unreliable. In order to avoid such unintentional bias, researchers may look back at reports written at the time about the child's development, for example medical or school records. These records will not be biased by subsequent outcome, but they may be scanty or deal with matters not of interest to the researcher. *Prospective studies* allow the researcher to decide which early behaviours to monitor, and are free from memory biases. However, if the disorder of interest is rare, an enormous initial sample may be needed in order to ensure that some of the infants will later prove to have the condition.

An early indicator of autism will only be useful if it is fairly specific and universal. One can think of this issue in terms of false alarms and misses. It is no good identifying a feature that many non-autistic children also show (e.g. preference for routine) – using this as an indicator will lead us to raise "false alarms", labelling "normal" children as autistic. Similarly, it is no good identifying a feature that only some children with autism show (e.g. disliking being touched) – this will lead to a large number of "misses", where autism is not picked up. While many parents of autistic children report that they suspected something to be wrong from the first months onward, this must be seen against the background of the parents of normal children who may also suspect problems (in their case unnecessarily). It may also be that what such parents are noticing in infancy is not the autism but the severe learning difficulties which their child may also have. The search for an early indicator of autism must therefore compare the early development of autistic children with the early development both of normal children and of children with severe learning difficulties but not autism.

At present, a number of studies are underway to investigate the earliest possible identification of autism. A follow-up study by Lister looked at whether problems at 12 months (as assessed by health visitors using a specially devised questionnaire) predict the triad of impairments at 12 years. Results from the initial cohort of 1208 infants, followed up at 6 and 12 years, suggest that nothing is picked up at 1 year which would differentiate those children who later receive a diagnosis of autism from those who do not (Lister 1992). Not only were no obvious markers of autism identified by health visitors in the child's first year, in addition abnormalities in social-communicative development at 12 months did not necessarily put a child at risk for later problems of this type.

A rather different approach has been taken by Johnson et al. (1992), who looked back at the infant health screening records of children who were subsequently diagnosed as suffering from autism, and compared them with

Table 3.1 Diagnostic criteria for autistic disorder from DSM-III-R.

At least 8 of the following 16 items are present, these to include at least two items from A, one from B, and one from C.

Note: Consider a criterion to be met only if the behaviour is abnormal for the person's developmental level.

A. Qualitative impairment in reciprocal social interaction as manifested by the following:

(The examples within parentheses are arranged so that those first mentioned are more likely to apply to younger or more handicapped, and the later ones, to older or less handicapped, persons with this disorder.)

1. marked lack of awareness of the existence or feelings of others (e.g. treats a person as if he or she were a piece of furniture; does not notice another person's distress; apparently has no concept of the need of others for privacy)

2. no or abnormal seeking of comfort at times of distress (e.g. does not come for comfort even when ill, hurt, or tired; seeks comfort in a stereotyped way, e.g. says "cheese, cheese, cheese" whenever hurt)

3. no or impaired imitation (e.g. does not wave bye-bye; does not copy mother's domestic activities; mechanical imitation of other's actions out of context)

4. no or abnormal social play (e.g. does not actively participate in simple games; prefers solitary play activities; involves other children in play only as "mechanical aids")

5. gross impairment in ability to make peer friendships (e.g. no interest in making peer friendships; despite interest in making friends, demonstrates lack of under-standing of conventions of social interaction, for example, reads phone book to uninterested peer)

B. Qualitative impairment in verbal and nonverbal communication, and in imaginative activity, as manifested by the following:

(The numbered items are arranged so that those first listed are more likely to apply to younger or more handicapped, and the later ones, to older or less handicapped, persons with this disorder.)

1. no mode of communication, such as communicative babbling, facial expression, gesture, mime, or spoken language

2. markedly abnormal nonverbal communication, as in the use of eye-to-eye gaze, facial expression, body posture, or gestures to initiate or modulate social interac-tion (e.g. does not anticipate being held, stiffens when held, does not look at the person or smile when making a social approach, does not greet parents or visitors, has a fixed stare in social situations)

3. absence of imaginative activity, such as playacting of adult roles, fantasy charac-ters, or animals; lack of interest in stories about imaginary events

4. marked abnormalities in the production of speech, including volume, pitch, stress,

rate, rhythm, and intonation (e.g. monotonous tone, questionlike melody, or high pitch)

5. marked abnormalities in the form or content of speech, including stereotyped and repetitive use of speech (e.g. immediate echolalia or mechanical repetition of television commercial); use of "you" when "I" is meant (e.g. using "You want cookie?" to mean "I want a cookie"); idiosyncratic use of words or phrases (e.g. "Go on green riding" to mean "I want to go on the swing"); or frequent irrelevant remarks (e.g. starts talking about train schedules during a conversation about sports)

6. marked impairment in the ability to initiate or sustain a conversation with others, despite adequate speech (e.g. indulging in lengthy monologues on one subject regardless of interjections from others)

C. *Markedly restricted repertoire of activities and interests, as manifested by the following:*

1. stereotyped body movements, e.g. hand-flicking or -twisting, spinning, head-banging, complex whole-body movements

2. persistent preoccupation with parts of objects (e.g. sniffing or smelling objects, repetitive feeling of texture of materials, spinning wheels of toy cars) or attachment to unusual objects (e.g. insists on carrying around a piece of string)

3. marked distress over changes in trivial aspects of environment, e.g. when a vase is moved from usual position

4. unreasonable insistence on following routines in precise detail, e.g. insisting that exactly the same route always be followed when shopping

5. markedly restricted range of interests and a preoccupation with one narrow interest, e.g. interested only in lining up objects, in amassing facts about meteorology, or in pretending to be a fantasy character

D. *Onset during infancy or childhood.*

Specify if childhood onset (after 36 months of age).

Source: American Psychiatric Association: *Diagnostic and statistical manual of mental disorders,* third edition, revised, Washington, DC, American Psychiatric Association, 1987.

the records of children who grew up to be "normal" or to have mild/moderate learning difficulties (but not autism). They found that the group with learning difficulties showed impairments in many of the areas tested (motor, vision, hearing and language) as assessed at their 12 month screening. By contrast, the autistic children had shown very few problems at this age. At their 18 month assessment, however, many of the infants who were later diagnosed autistic showed problems in social development. While a few of the learning difficulties children also showed social problems at 18 months, these were part of a more general delay across all areas of functioning. In the autistic children, by contrast, social deficits were noticed by the health visitors in the absence of other problems. This study suggests that it is not until some time in the second year that autistic children show social impairments – at 12 months the children in this study were judged to be normally sociable by health visitors (on items such as smiling and responsiveness to people).

Other studies have explored possible early indicators of autism through rather different techniques. Single case studies have been reported, concerning children who for one reason or another were closely monitored in their early years, before autism was suspected (e.g. Sparling 1991). Home movies may also be a good source of information about the early years of an autistic child's development (Adrien et al. 1991). Both types of study so far suggest very early but rather subtle abnormalities, however the lack of control subjects makes it hard to know which, if any, of these early features might be specific to autism. It remains a possibility that early problems are due merely to attendant learning difficulties, or that the developmental histories of many "normal" children may also contain reports of similar odd behaviours.

The most ambitious study to date trying to establish the earliest indicators of autism is a prospective study currently underway in Britain and Sweden. Baron-Cohen et al. (1992) overcame the problem of doing prospective research with a rare disorder, by targeting a group of infants who were particularly likely to have autism. Since autism appears to have a genetic component (see Ch. 4), these researchers concentrated their attentions on the siblings of children with autism. They devised a screening schedule, the Checklist for Autism in Toddlers (CHAT), based on current theories of the behavioural and cognitive characteristics of autism (see Ch. 5). In particular, the checklist focused on pretend play, joint-attention and pointing, social interest and social play. The CHAT was used by doctors and health visitors to screen 41 18-month-olds, all of whom had an older brother or sister with autism. A comparison group of 50 randomly selected 18-month-olds was also screened using the CHAT. More than 80 per cent of the control group passed all items, showing normal development of imaginative and social abilities at 18 months. No child from the control group showed problems in more than one of the five key areas. By contrast, four of the 41 high-risk children failed on two or more of the key items. Follow-up at 30 months found that these four children, and only these four, had received a diagnosis of autism. This study, then, suggests that we may be able to detect autism at 18 months by looking for deficits in specific areas of social, communicative and imaginative competence. The significance of this preliminary finding for our psychological theories of autism is discussed further in Chapter 6.

Epidemiology

The recorded incidence of autism in the population depends crucially upon how it is diagnosed and defined. The incidence in most studies appears to be around 4–10 autistic children in every 10,000 live births. However, Wing & Gould (1979) reported an incidence of 21 per 10,000 for "the triad of social, language and behavioural impairments" in the Camberwell study. Gillberg et al. (1986) found similarly high rates of the triad and mental handicap in Swedish teenagers. Other studies report an incidence of around 10 per 10,000 (Bryson et al. 1988, Tanoue et al. 1988, Ciadella & Mamelle 1989). These recent studies (from America, Japan and France, respectively) suggest that autism is found throughout the world, and is not more common in any one society than in others. While the reported incidence of autism has increased in recent years, this is probably due to better information and a wider conception of autism.

All the epidemiological studies show a significantly greater number of boys than girls with autism. Male to female ratios vary from 2:1 (Ciadella & Mamelle 1989) to almost 3:1 (Steffenburg & Gillberg 1986). The sex ratio seems to vary with ability: most girls with autism are at the lower end of the ability range, while at the more able end ("Asperger's syndrome") boys may out-number girls 5:1 (Lord & Schopler 1987). Szatmari & Jones (1991) have suggested some possible reasons for the lower IQ of females with autism; for example, females may be more strongly affected by the autism gene or there may be genetic heterogeneity, with more "mild" forms (incomplete penetrance) of disorder being X linked and hence more common in boys.

Both Kanner (1943) and Asperger (1944) remarked on the intelligence and high social standing of the families of children with autism, and this has given rise to the idea that autism is more prevalent among the higher socio-economic classes. There is little support for such an idea – of the many epidemiological and population-based studies of autism, only one to date (Lotter 1966) has shown any evidence of a social class bias. A number of reports have suggested that the association with social class may be an artifact caused by, for example, the greater likelihood that a middle-class parent will be able to get their child seen by a specialist (Wing 1980, Gillberg & Schaumann 1982).

The association of autism with major organic conditions, with severe learning difficulties and with epilepsy is discussed in Chapter 4, where the biological basis of autism is considered.

Conclusions

It is the behaviour of people with autism which can be observed and must be coped with directly. Therefore, it is clearly important to know about the behavioural nature of autism. Behavioural techniques for managing autism can be very effective (for a review, see Schreibman 1988). However, we can gain insight into these behaviours and better understand their cause and nature if we also know about autism at the cognitive level. Chapters 5 and 6 consider this aspect of our understanding of autism. The next chapter focuses on the biological impairments in autism which underlie the behavioural and cognitive features of this disorder.

Suggested reading

Rutter, M. & E. Schopler 1987. Autism and pervasive developmental disorders: conceptual and diagnostic issues. *Journal of Autism and Developmental Disorders* **17**, 159–86.

Wing, L. 1988. The continuum of autistic characteristics. In *Diagnosis and assessment in autism*, E. Schopler & G. B. Mesibov (eds), 91–110. New York: Plenum Press.

Chapter 4

Autism at the biological level

The psychogenic myth

Bettelheim (1956, 1967) was the source of the "refrigerator mother" theory – the idea that children become autistic as a maladaptive response to a threatening and unloving environment. This idea was later taken up by Kanner, who believed he saw mild autistic features (e.g. detachment and social difficulty) in the parents of the children he treated. Originally, however, Kanner had interpreted these traits as signs of a genetic component to autism (Kanner 1943). This early insight has proved correct (see below), while no evidence has emerged to support the psychogenic explanations of autism. Against psychogenic theories is the fact that cases of children who are mistreated to a horrifying degree and neglected almost entirely show that such a history does not give rise to autism (Clarke & Clarke 1976). For example, Genie – a young girl who was discovered after having spent the first 13 years of her life tied to a chair and left in virtual isolation by her parents – quickly made social ties with those who cared for her after she was rescued (Curtiss 1977).

While the psychogenic explanation of autism is now discredited with most researchers and clinicians in Britain, the effects of this cruel myth are still felt by parents. Mothers are still made to feel responsible for their child's difficulties by misinformed doctors and writers in this country, and in parts of Europe this untenable view still holds sway over the diagnosis and treatment of children with autism.

Evidence for an organic cause

Reviews of the biology of autism conclude that evidence for an organic cause is overwhelming (Coleman & Gillberg 1985, Schopler & Mesibov 1987, C. Gillberg 1991). A recent study by Steffenburg (1991), for example, found that almost 90 per cent of her sample (of 35 autistic and 17 autistic-like children) showed some evidence of brain damage or dysfunction. She presents the pie-chart in Figure 4.1 to show the relative incidence of different sorts of brain abnormalities in her sample.

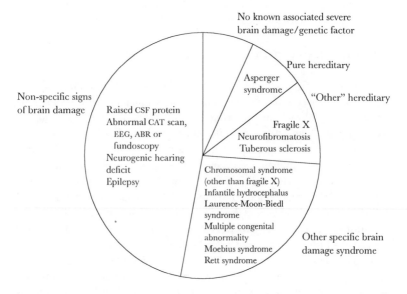

Figure 4.1 Incidence of different types of brain abnormality in Steffenburg's (1991) sample. ABR, auditory brainstem response; CAT, computerized axial tomography; CSF, cerebrospinal fluid; EEG, electroencephalogram. (By kind permission of the author and publisher.)

One indication that brain damage is at the root of autism is the high incidence of epilepsy in autistic children (Olsson et al. 1988). Another is the tendency for general mental handicap to accompany autism: around three-quarters of all people with autism are also mentally handicapped (i.e. have an IQ below 70), and as one looks at groups of people with progressively lower IQ the incidence of autism increases (Smalley et al. 1988). This could be easily explained by a model in which autism results from damage to a circumscribed brain region or pathway, call it X. Widespread damage to the brain, such as causes mental retardation, will be more likely to knock out the specific component X the more of the brain it affects. While no unambiguous and universal findings have emerged to suggest the site of the lesion, or the precise nature of the neurochemical pathway disrupted in autism, we can be confident that autism has a primary cause at the level of the brain (Steffenburg & Gillberg 1990).

Is autism hereditary?

Evidence for a genetic component in autism is weighty, although the exact rôle of the child's genes is far from clear (Rutter et al. 1990). The sex ratio in autism is suggestive. As mentioned in Chapter 3, autism is more than twice as common in boys as in girls (Lotter 1966), and this ratio increases to 5:1 at the high-ability end of the autism spectrum (Lord & Schopler 1987). There is a significant familial loading for autism: autism is 50 times more frequent in the siblings of autistic people than in the population at large (Smalley et al. 1988). Siblings who are not themselves autistic show a much increased incidence of other cognitive impairments, such as language disorders and social impairments (August et al. 1981, Bolton & Rutter 1990). Monozygotic (identical) twins also have a far higher concordance for autism than dizygotic (fraternal) twins (Folstein & Rutter 1977), showing that familial loading is not simply due to a mother's tendency to experience difficult pregnancies.

However, the concordance even in identical twins is not perfect; it is possible to be the identical twin of someone with autism, and yet not be autistic. One possibility is that there may be a genetic predisposition for autism, which is only fulfilled if triggered by pre- or perinatal difficulties. Mothers of autistic children report more problems during pregnancy and delivery than mothers of, for example, children who later develop schizophrenia (Green et al. 1984). Folstein & Rutter (1977) also found that where monozygotic twins were discordant for autism (i.e. only one twin was affected), the twin with autism was the twin who had experienced a difficult delivery. The exact rôle which such pre- and perinatal problems play, however, is still unclear – some authors (e.g. Goodman 1990) have suggested that they may be a result (rather than a cause) of abnormalities in the child.

The incidence of cognitive and social-communicative impairments in

29

the non-autistic siblings of children with autism (August et al. 1981) has led to the suggestion of an "extended phenotype" of autism (see also Ch. 10). It is possible, then, that the gene responsible for autism may in some cases produce far milder handicaps. Szatmari & Jones (1991) have recently discussed the types of inheritance that might be involved in autism. They conclude that cases of autism might be divided into three aetiological groups: exogenous (caused by external factors such as prenatal accidents); autosomal recessive (carried on non-sex chromosomes, but only expressed if present in a double dose – i.e. inherited from both father and mother); X linked (carried on the female sex chromosome). However, they stress that more data need to be collected concerning the pattern of occurrence of autism in families and the severity of attendant general learning difficulties, in order to explore the possible modes of inheritance.

A final common pathway

A general consensus at present is that a number of rather different biological causes may result in autism (Schopler & Mesibov 1987, Gillberg & Coleman 1992). Fragile X syndrome, phenylketonuria, and tuberous sclerosis (all of which are genetically caused) each carry an increased risk of autism (Gillberg & Forsell 1984, Blomquist et al. 1985, Reiss et al. 1986, Hunt & Dennis 1987). In some tragic cases, herpes simplex encephalitis has left in its wake severely autistic behaviour in a previously normal adolescent (Gillberg 1986) or adult (I. C. Gillberg 1991). It would seem, then, that we may think in terms of a "final common pathway": all these different disorders and factors (birth trauma, genetic abnormality, etc.) may affect the same specific component of the brain, resulting in autism. Aitken (1991: 932) concludes that, "It would seem to be the developmental timing of the insult, and hence the disruption to a critical phase in neurogenesis, which is important in the development of autism, and not the specific nature of the causative agent".

Unfortunately, no agreement has yet emerged concerning the critical area or pathway of the brain which is damaged in autism. Localizing higher cognitive functions (such as the social, communication and imagination skills impaired in autism) is always problematic. To date a number of different brain regions have been suggested as the site of damage, including the cerebellum (involved in motor coordination) and the limbic system (involved in emotion regulation).

Autopsy studies, usually involving only a handful of subjects, have provided some evidence of abnormalities in the cerebellum, including significant reductions in Purkinje cell density compared with normal controls (Ritvo et al. 1986). Bauman & Kemper (1985), in a single case study of a severely mentally handicapped and epileptic man with autism, found abnormalities in the hippocampus, parts of the amygdala, and cerebellum, compared with a normal age-matched male subject. Without data from the brains of non-autistic people with learning difficulties (mental handicap), however, data from any but normally intelligent autistic subjects are hard to interpret. The possibility remains that autopsy studies have pinpointed brain abnormalities which are associated not with autism itself but with attendant mental handicap. The effects on brain tissue of medication, or even of a lifetime of "autistic behaviour" (motor stereotypy, etc.), are also unknown – making conclusions about the causal rôle of any discovered abnormalities particularly complex.

In vivo brain-imaging techniques using radioactive substances or magnetic resonance imaging (MRI) to map the brain have been used to look for structural abnormalities. A number of studies using computerized axial tomography (CAT) scanning of autistic individuals have found abnormalities (e.g. increased ventricular dilation, Campbell et al. 1982) which have not been replicated in subsequent samples (Creasey et al. 1986). Other studies have found significant abnormalities which are not, however, specific to autism (Ballotin et al. 1989). A number of MRI scan studies provide some evidence of cerebellar abnormalities. Courchesne et al. (1987, 1988) have found abnormalities in the cerebellar vermis of relatively able individuals with autism. Although it has been argued that the cerebellum contributes to normal cognitive functions (Leiner et al. 1986), it is not clear how abnormalities in this area could be directly tied to the very specific pattern of cognitive and behavioural deficits and skills found in autism.

More recently, many researchers, discouraged by the failure to find any obvious "hole in the head" which is unique and universal to autism, have begun to look for the site of damage with neuropsychological test batteries. Currently popular is the idea that the frontal lobes may be implicated in autism, based on the finding that autistic subjects tend to do poorly on tasks which adults with acquired lesions to the frontal lobes also fail (Rumsey & Hamburger 1988, Prior & Hoffman 1990, Ozonoff et al. 1991a). However, it would be premature to conclude that people with autism and individuals with frontal lobe damage necessarily fail these tasks for the same reasons. Failure on frontal lobe tasks need not indicate damage to the frontal lobes in autism: the frontal lobes cover a large area of the brain which takes inputs from many other cortical and subcortical regions. The picture is further complicated by the fact that performance on certain arrays of supposedly "frontal" tasks does not necessarily correlate well, and that patients can be found who clearly show loss of frontal tissue in brain scans, but still perform well on these tasks, in addition to patients who fail despite no obvious damage to these brain areas (Shallice & Burgess 1991). Recent theories about the nature of the autistic cognitive impairment which take as their starting point failure on frontal tasks are discussed in Chapter 6.

The search for the area of the brain which is damaged in autism is likely to be greatly facilitated in the future by the development of increasingly advanced brain imaging techniques. While structural imaging (e.g. CAT, MRI) gives a picture of the anatomy of the brain, functional imaging (positron emission tomography or PET, and in the future MRI also) shows the pattern of activity of the brain when the subject is engaged in particular tasks (e.g. reading, memorizing, etc.). With the increasingly sophisticated techniques of functional imaging, using our knowledge of autism at the behavioural and cognitive levels, it may become possible to locate the area of the brain which is damaged in autism.

Conclusions

Whereas much research has been conducted into the biological nature of autism, and much has been learnt about the genetics and predisposing medical conditions, relatively little has been conclusively determined regarding the actual brain area or pathway involved. We are still a long way from pinpointing the area of damage in the autistic *brain*, but it may be that we can specify what function is lost in the autistic *mind*. With increasingly sophisticated functional brain imaging it may be that psychological research will be as important as biological research in locating the brain abnormality specific to autism. Chapters 5 and 6 look at some answers to the question "What is autism?" at the cognitive level.

Suggested reading

Bolton, P. & M. Rutter 1990. Genetic influences in autism. *International Review of Psychiatry* **2**, 67–80.

Gillberg, C. & M. A. Coleman 1992. *The biology of the autistic syndromes*, 2nd edn. New York: Praeger.

Schopler, E. & G. B. Mesibov (eds) 1987. *Neurobiological issues in autism*. New York: Plenum Press.

Chapter 5

Autism at the cognitive level: understanding minds

Good and bad theories

What work must a theory do for us? How can a theory open our eyes to facts, and how can we avoid being blinded by our preconceived notions?

A good theory must do a number of things:
- it must make concrete predictions, which can be tested;
- it must go beyond the evidence, and do more than describe;
- it must be specific and yet fit with what we know generally.

So a good theory of autism must:
- generate ways of testing the theory;
- give a causal account;
- explain the specific pattern of deficits and abilities in autism;
- fit with what we know about normal development.

If several symptoms co-occur reliably the most simple explanation is that they are caused by the same underlying deficit. Impairments in socialization, communication and imagination cohere (Wing & Gould 1979). It has been suggested that a single cognitive deficit could underlie these three diverse features of autism.

Looking again at the triad

In Chapter 3 the claim was made that autism is characterized by a triad of impairments – problems in socialization, communication and imagination.

However, each of these three areas is itself made up of a great variety of different behaviours, which rely on different cognitive mechanisms, and which emerge at different points in normal development. The task faced by cognitive theories of autism is to explain the specific pattern of deficits and preserved abilities across these three areas in autism. So before reviewing one current theory of autism at the cognitive level, it may be useful to look again at the specific nature of the triad of impairments.

Socialization

Autistic children are not globally impaired in social functioning. For example, autistic children seem to show attachment behaviours which are no different from those of other (non-autistic) children with severe learning difficulties (of the same mental age) (Shapiro et al. 1987, Sigman & Mundy 1989). Similarly, autistic children know about their physical identity – they can recognize themselves in a mirror at the normal mental age (Dawson & McKissick 1984). They are also as good as controls of the same verbal ability at recognizing the faces of others (Ozonoff et al. 1990, Smalley & Asarnow 1990). Autistic people are able to respond differentially to different people and to different types of approach (Clarke & Rutter 1981). Many autistic children are not pervasively aloof, and do show proximity-seeking behaviours and vocalizations for social attention (Sigman et al. 1986, Sigman & Mundy 1989).

Against this backdrop of mental-age appropriate social behaviours, autistic children show a specific pattern of impairments in social understanding. There is some disagreement as to the age at which these difficulties first emerge – as yet autism is rarely reliably diagnosed before the age of 3 years. As a result, social behaviours which are shown by the normally developing infant have not been explored in infants with autism – rather, these abilities have been examined in older autistic children, or even adults.

(a) Autistic children show an inability to *share and direct attention* – they do not point to things in order to share their focus of interest (so-called "protodeclarative" pointing, Curcio 1978). By contrast, normal children from around 9–12 months will follow an adult's point or eye gaze, to share their focus of attention.

(b) There may be a specific problem with *imitation*. There is some evidence that even newborn normal infants show imitation – they will stick out their tongues to an adult making this face, and open their mouths to an open-mouthed adult (Meltzoff & Moore 1977, Meltzoff 1988).

35

Autistic adults and children seem to have difficulty in copying movements (Sigman & Ungerer 1984, Hertzig et al. 1989). However, these studies involved copying more or less complex body movements, and do not tell us about the autistic infant's ability to show the primitive imitation normally seen in neonates.

(c) Autistic people seem to have impaired *recognition of affect*. Again, the first evidence of sensitivity to affect appears very early in normal development: there is some ability to discriminate between emotions at 2–4 months (Field et al. 1982), and by 7 months infants can correctly match emotional sounds to emotional pictures (Walker 1982). At 12 months babies show "social referencing" – responding differently to a new toy according to the mother's facial expression (disgust or fear versus smiling) (Hornik et al. 1987). A number of studies have suggested deficits in the recognition of emotion by autistic children, although, again, subjects tend to be aged 5 years or older (Hobson 1986a,b, Hertzig et al. 1989, Macdonald et al. 1989, Smalley & Asarnow 1990). However, there has been some suggestion that autistic subjects do not show specific problems if compared to controls of the same language level (Ozonoff et al. 1990).

Communication

The range of communication handicaps in the autistic spectrum is very striking – from the totally mute autistic child who does not use even gesture to communicate, through the echolalic child who may parrot whole sentences which appear to have no relation to the context, or the autistic child who will use single words inflexibly as requests, to the fluently speaking but pragmatically bizarre child with Asperger's syndrome. A great deal of research has been conducted into this range of manifestations of the autistic communication impairment (for a review, see Frith 1989b, also Tager-Flusberg 1981, Schopler & Mesibov 1985, Paul 1987). Some of the language problems which emerge as specific to autism (and not due merely to developmental delay, or to superimposed additional specific language impairment) include the following:

– delay or lack of development of speech, without any compensating gesture;
– failure to respond to others' speech (e.g. the child doesn't orient to his own name);
– stereotyped and repetitive use of language;

- pronoun reversal (saying "you" for "I");
- idiosyncratic use of words, and appearance of neologisms;
- failure to initiate or sustain conversation normally;
- abnormalities of prosody (pitch, stress, intonation);
- semantic/conceptual difficulties;
- abnormal non-verbal communication (gesture, facial expression).

As in the case of socialization, not all areas of language are equally affected in autism. For example, those children who speak usually show fairly normal phonology and grammar. What seems most deviant is the autistic child's *use* of language, that is, his pragmatic competence (e.g. Baltaxe 1977). So, for example, a child may show over-literal interpretation of language, like the intelligent autistic boy who, when told "stick your coat anywhere", asked in all earnestness for some glue.

Imagination

Autistic children show a striking absence of spontaneous pretend or "symbolic" play (Wulff 1985). So, while the normal 2-year-old will pretend that a toy brick is a car, and happily drive, park, and even crash the pretend car, an autistic child (even of a much higher mental age) will simply mouth, throw or spin the block. Pretend play seems to be replaced in autism by repetitive activities, which may become obsessional; the child may line up objects in a certain arrangement that must not be interfered with, or may spin all objects which he can get his hands on. In adults with autism the same lack of imagination may be shown in a rather different way. For example, adults with autism, even those of high IQ, show little interest in fiction in the form of TV soap operas, novels or films. In general there is a great preference for facts, and the obsessive functional play of the young autistic child may give way to obsessional interests in, for example, railway timetables, dates of birth, bus routes, and so on. The special nature of these interests comes not so much from their content (not every rail enthusiast is autistic!), but from their circumscribed and narrow nature. So, for example, the autistic man who had learnt the name of every type of carrot (apparently there are around 50!), showed no particular interest in growing or eating carrots. Similarly, the young autistic man who asked everyone he met about the door colour of the juvenile magistrates courts in their area, when asked why he did not inquire about the adult courts said, "They bore me to tears!".

The "theory of mind" account; an example of the work theories can do

One psychological theory in particular has aroused a great deal of interest over the last 5 years, and has so far proved extremely successful at predicting and explaining the universal and specific features of autism. Uta Frith, Alan Leslie and Simon Baron-Cohen have suggested that the triad of behavioural handicaps in autism result from an impairment of the fundamental human ability to "mind-read". Normal children, from around the age of 4 years, understand (however implicitly) that people have beliefs and desires about the world, and that it is these mental states (rather than the physical state of the world) which determine a person's behaviour. The "theory of mind" explanation of autism suggests that autistic people lack this ability to think about thoughts, and so are specifically impaired in certain (but not all) social, communicative and imaginative skills. Baron-Cohen et al. (1985) followed Premack & Woodruff's (1978) definition of the "sexy" but misleading phrase, "theory of mind": to have a theory of mind is to be able to attribute independent mental states to self and others in order to explain and predict behaviour. As might befit a "theory" which was first ascribed to chimpanzees (Premack & Woodruff 1978), theory of mind was thought of not as a conscious theory but as an innately given cognitive mechanism allowing a special sort of representation – the representation of mental states. The rest of this chapter explores the theory of mind account of autism in some detail, as one example of how a cognitive theory can help us to understand a behaviourally diagnosed and biologically caused syndrome such as autism. In Chapter 6 some alternative psychological theories of autism are considered.

Background

This theory began with the observation that autistic children do not spontaneously engage in pretend play. As Alan Leslie (1987) has pointed out, pretence is an extraordinarily complex behaviour to emerge so early in normal development. During the second year of life, just as the child is learning, for example, what a telephone is, that bananas are good to eat, and the names for these things, mother may suddenly pick up a banana and hold it to her ear, saying, "Look, mummy's on the telephone!" This is no way to teach a child about bananas and telephones! The child should be upset, confused; instead he is delighted. Around 18 months the normal child can understand and indulge in pretend play (Fein 1981) – how is this possible without wrecking the child's encyclopaedic world knowledge?

Leslie (1987, 1988) has suggested that in order to prevent the interference of pretence with real-world knowledge, the child must possess two types of representation. Pretence is, for Leslie, good evidence that the 2-year-old has not only *primary representations* of things as they really are in the world (with a premium on accuracy and truth), but also *metarepresentations* which are used to capture pretending. Leslie suggests that metarepresentations contain four elements:

> agent – informational relation – referent – "expression"
> e.g. mother – pretends – of this banana – "it is a telephone".

The expression is placed in decoupling marks (" ") in Leslie's scheme to indicate that it is kept separate from reality (as represented in primary representations).

Leslie hypothesized that autistic individuals, who show impairments in spontaneous pretence, have a specific impairment in forming metarepresentations. This would be a circular argument, except that metarepresentations are necessary for more than just pretence – they are vital for representing other "informational relations" or propositional attitudes (mental states), such as "think", "hope", "intend", "wish" and "believe".

This hypothesis, that autistic individuals lack metarepresentations and so are unable to think about mental states, generated a testable prediction about the social handicap in autism. If autistic children do not show pretence because they cannot form metarepresentations, then they should also be incapable of understanding other mental states. They will be, in effect, "mind-blind", while others are able to "mind-read" – attributing mental states in order to understand behaviour.

While it is clear that autistic children show social impairments, proving that they lack understanding of mental states (such as "think" and "believe") requires a precise test. Research into the nature of the social deficit in autism has therefore been greatly helped by recent work on the normal development of social competence, and specifically by the study of the child's so-called "theory of mind".

Evidence for the theory

The term "theory of mind" refers to the ability to attribute independent mental states to oneself and others, in order to explain behaviour. These mental states must be independent both of the real world state of affairs (because people can believe things which are not true), and independent of the mental states other people have (because you and I can believe, want, and pretend different things from one another). The philosopher Daniel Dennett pointed out that only understanding and predicting a character's behaviour based on a *false* belief could show theory of mind conclusively, since otherwise the real state of affairs (or the subject's own convictions) could be appealed to without the need to postulate mental states at all (Dennett 1978). Such a strict test of the ability to represent mental states was exactly what was needed to test the "mind-blindness" theory of autism.

Baron-Cohen et al. (1985) explored the prediction that autistic children lack a "theory of mind" (i.e. the ability to "mentalize" or "mind-read"). They tested 20 autistic children with mental ages well over 4 years on the now-classic Sally–Ann task, a simple version of a false belief task devised by Wimmer & Perner (1983) (Fig. 5.1). In this task the child is shown two dolls, one called Sally, and one called Ann; Sally has a basket and Ann has a box. The child watches as Sally places her marble in the basket and goes out. While she's out, naughty Ann moves Sally's marble from the basket to her own box, then she goes out. Now Sally comes back in. The child is asked the test question, "Where will Sally look for her marble?" Baron-Cohen et al. found that 80% (16/20) of the autistic children failed to appreciate Sally's false belief – instead of saying that Sally would look in the basket where she put the marble, they said that she would look in the box, where the marble really was. In contrast, 86% of children with Down's syndrome (12/14) of rather lower mental age succeeded on the task, appreciating Sally's false belief. Normal young children of 4 years also understand the false belief in the Sally–Ann task.

It seems then that children with autism may have a specific and unique problem with understanding that people have mental states which can be different from the state of the real world and different from the autistic person's own mental state. Such a deficit, Frith (1989a) suggests, could account for their triad of impairments in socialization, communication and imagination. The causal model (from Frith 1992) illustrating this theory is shown in Figure 5.2.

This finding has now been replicated in a number of studies, using real people instead of toys, using a "think" question rather than a "look" question, and using a control group of specifically language-impaired children to rule out a language deficit explanation (Leslie & Frith 1988, Perner et al. 1989). People with autism have been shown to fail other false belief tasks,

Figure 5.1 The Sally–Ann task (by kind permission of the artist, Axel Scheffler). Reprinted from Frith 1989a.

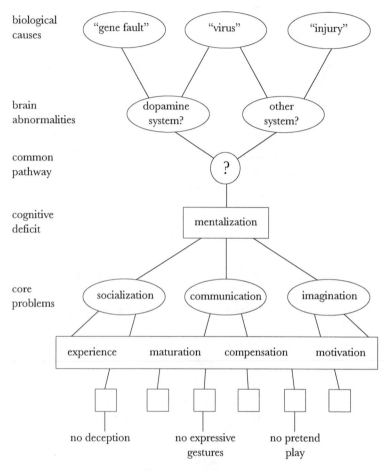

Figure 5.2 A causal model of the theory of mind account of autism (from Frith 1992, by kind permission of the author).

such as the "Smarties task" (Perner et al. 1989). In the Smarties task (Fig. 5.3) the child is asked to guess what a closed Smartie tube contains. Having answered "sweets" or "Smarties" the tube is opened to show the real contents, a pencil. The lid is then replaced and the child asked, "When Billy comes in, I'm going to show him this tube, closed up like I showed it to you. I'm going to ask him what he thinks is inside. What will he say?" In this task, which normal 4-year-olds pass, autistic children again fail to recognize

Figure 5.3 The Smarties task (by kind permission of the artist, Axel Scheffler). Reprinted from Frith 1989a.

that Billy will have a false belief.

The power of this theory of autism is that it has predictions which are both specific and far-reaching enough to fit the clinical picture of autism (Frith 1989a). In particular, it can explain not only the handicaps of autism, but also the preservation of some functions. It predicts that any skill which requires only primary representations should be unimpaired in autism – thus allowing for the islets of ability, good rote memory, savant abilities, and above-average IQ sometimes seen in autism. Other theories have to meet this challenge. The theory of mind explanation of autism has allowed researchers to make clear cuts between what appeared to be very similar behaviours – carving nature at the joints according to a precise theory about the underlying cognitive "bone structure". For example, Attwood et al. (1988) found that the autistic child's well known absence of gestures actually applied only to those gestures which normally influence *mental states* (e.g. expressions of consolation, embarrassment and goodwill), whereas children with autism showed as many gestures which manipulate *behaviour* (e.g. signals to come, be quiet or go away) as did control subjects with severe learning difficulties. Similarly, Baron-Cohen (1989a) found that autistic subjects were impaired in their use and understanding of pointing for the sake of sharing attention (protodeclarative pointing) but not of pointing in order to get a desired object (protoimperative pointing). Other fine cuts have been made between, for example, understanding seeing versus understanding knowing (Perner et al. 1989, Baron-Cohen 1992), and recognizing happiness versus recognizing surprise (Baron-Cohen et al. 1993a). Such distinctions in the smooth continuum of everyday behaviour would appear to be hard to derive from or explain by other psychological theories of autism (e.g. primary emotional deficits or motivational problems). Chapter 6 considers the advantages and drawbacks of some alternative psychological theories of autism.

Are autistic individuals just like 3-year-olds?

False belief tasks, such as the Sally–Ann test, have become important in the study of autism. However, such tasks are also used with normally developing children, to explore the development of social understanding in the pre-school years. From Wimmer & Perner (1983) onwards, most researchers have found that it is not until the age of 4 years that the normally developing child passes standard false belief tasks. A great deal of debate surrounds this finding, both interpreting the implications for theory, and discussing the details of the experiments. The tasks can be simplified in a number of ways (e.g. asking where Sally will look *first*, Siegal & Beattie 1991; using a hide and seek context, Freeman et al. 1991; or tagging the child's belief using an external representation such as a photograph of the expected contents in the Smarties task, Mitchell & Lacohée 1991), and these modifications improve the performance of 3-year-olds. However, the finding remains that standard false belief tasks are difficult for children under 4 years. This finding has even been replicated among the children of the Baka people in the rainforests of the Cameroon (Avis & Harris 1991), suggesting that the understanding of actions in terms of mental states is universal and not simply culturally imposed.

If normal 3-year-olds, like most subjects with autism, fail standard false belief tasks, is it true to say that people with autism are simply delayed in their development of theory of mind, stuck at a 3-year-old level? Probably not, for a number of reasons. First, 3-year-olds show a number of behaviours which demonstrate their understanding of *true* beliefs and of the mental world. Normal 3-year-olds are well able to talk about internal states (happy, like, want), and use not only idiomatic phrases including mental state terms (e.g. "don't know"), but also genuine references to mental contents (e.g. "she doesn't *know* all this" referring to an absent child) (Bretherton & Beeghley 1982, Shatz et al. 1983). In addition, 3-year-olds understand that looking leads to knowing (Pratt & Bryant 1990), which autistic children fail to comprehend (Perner et al. 1989). Secondly, normally-developing 3-year-olds will have shown a spontaneous ability to understand and engage in pretend play since their second year. In experimental tests, 3-year-olds are able to distinguish real versus pretend entities (Wellman & Estes 1986). In this respect they are very different indeed from individuals with autism, who fail to show spontaneous pretence, and do not make normal pretend–real distinctions in tests (Baron-Cohen 1989a).

If normally developing 3-year-olds can understand pretend play, giving good evidence of the ability to form metarepresentations, what holds them back from passing standard false belief tasks? There is much argument in the literature about this (see, for example, Astington & Gopnik 1991) but there seems good reason to believe that they fail the Sally–Ann task for rather different reasons from children with autism. Roth & Leslie (1991), in a cleverly designed experiment looking at attribution of mental states in comprehension of a deceptive utterance, showed clear differences between autistic subjects and 3-year-old children. They asked subjects about the beliefs of two story characters in a version of the Sally–Ann task. In this version, Sally returns and, before looking for her chocolate, asks Ann where it is. Ann tells a lie, saying the chocolate is in the dog's kennel. Now the child is asked, "Where does Ann think the chocolate is?" and, "Where does Sally think the chocolate is?", along with the standard memory and reality control questions. Three-year-old children in this experiment demonstrated some understanding of minds – they said that Ann believed what she said, and that Sally too would believe it. So although they failed to comprehend

45

the intended deception (which 4-year-olds recognized), they did in fact attribute a false belief. By contrast, the subjects with autism took no account of the characters' mental states at all, giving reality-based answers to both questions (Ann and Sally think the chocolate is where it really is – in Ann's box). This experiment elegantly demonstrates that, while 3-year-olds' understanding of minds may not be complete, it is qualitatively different from the lack of insight shown by most people with autism.

Representations in the mind and representations on paper

Is the autistic child's difficulty with understanding mental states simply part of a larger problem with understanding representations? Metarepresent-ation, as Alan Leslie has used the term, refers to a specific four-part rela-tion between an agent and his/her propositional attitude to a representation of some aspect of the world. His hypothesis, then, is that autistic children have difficulty representing *mental* representations, i.e. thoughts or mental states. However, how can we be sure that their problems are confined to the contents of heads? Do autistic children represent other types of represen-tations?

There are many types of representation outside the head, for example culturally-used representations such as pictures, photos and maps. A number of recent studies have explored autistic subjects' understanding of these non-mental representations. Leslie & Thaiss (1992), for example, com-pared understanding of an out-of-date belief (as in the Sally–Ann task) and understanding of an out-of-date photograph. For the photo task, pictured in Figure 5.4, the child was shown how to use a Polaroid instant camera. Then the child saw a character take a picture of a toy cat sitting on a chair. The photograph was taken from the camera and placed face down on the table to develop. Meanwhile, the toy cat was moved from the chair to the bed. The child was then asked the test question, "In the photo, where is the cat sitting?", as well as control questions about the original and current locations. This task was designed to be formally equivalent to the false belief task, but instead of Sally having a false (out-of-date) belief about the loca-tion of her marble, here the representation in question is not Sally's belief but a photograph.

The results showed that while less than 70 per cent of the 4-year-old children passed the photograph task, 100 per cent of the autistic subjects understood that the photograph showed a no-longer-actual scene. This success contrasted strikingly with the same subjects' performance on the

Figure 5.4 The false photograph task (by kind permission of the artist, Axel Scheffler).

Sally–Ann task ("Where does Sally think the marble is?"): only 23 per cent of the autistic group (mean age 12 years, mean verbal mental age 6 years) understood that Sally's belief was now out-of-date. By contrast the 4-year-olds had little difficulty with this task (over 70 per cent passed). In other words, non-mental representations such as photographs seem to pose no problem to children with autism. Their competence has also been demonstrated with "false" maps (Leslie & Thaiss 1992), shown in an independent study with "false" photographs (Leekam & Perner 1991), and found using "false" drawings (Charman & Baron-Cohen 1992).

Interestingly, normal 3-year-olds have great difficulty with the "false" photograph task (Zaitchik 1990). This may suggest that it is some general processing problem, such as difficulty with inhibition of perceptually salient information, which leads to their failure on false belief tasks, rather than any specific difficulty with understanding mental states. By contrast, since autistic children do well on the photograph task – which parallels formally the false belief task – it seems unlikely that extraneous task factors could account for the theory of mind task failure of this group of subjects. These experiments raise the exciting possibility that some autistic individuals might be able to use their intact knowledge of non-mental representations to supplement their impaired understanding of mental representations, thoughts and feelings. A preliminary study of self-report of inner experience by three very able people with autism (or "Asperger's syndrome") found that these subjects described their mental contents entirely in terms of pictures in the head (Hurlburt et al. 1994). This contrasted with reports from normal subjects using the same technique, who described a mixture of inner speech, pictures and "pure thought" (with no words or images present to awareness) (Hurlburt 1990). Intriguingly, in this small group of subjects with autism, ability to report inner experience in terms of images related closely to performance on standard theory of mind tasks, independent of IQ. This raises the possibility that these subjects used their understanding of external representations such as pictures to come to some understanding of mental representations such as beliefs.

"Mind-blindness": practical implications

Could the capacity to understand mental states be the single cognitive component at fault in autism? The ability to "mind-read" may be of such evolutionary importance that it is performed by a special, innately determined part of the brain. Could it be that the symptoms of autism follow from the lack of such a module? Certainly, an inability to form metarepresentations, and the consequent inability to reflect on the mental states of self and others, would have far-reaching effects on behaviour. The triad of impairments seen in autism could well be due to such an inability to "mentalize" (Frith et al. 1991): the inability to pretend generated the model, the social impairment would follow from a lack of appreciation of people as agents with independent minds, and the characteristic communicative impairments would follow from an inability to represent intentions, or recognize utterances as interpretations of a speaker's thoughts (see Ch. 7).

The mind-blindness theory seems able to explain the triad, but does it have practical implications for the care and education of people with autism? Can we use this theory to "get inside the mind" of a person with autism?

> Imagine yourself alone in a foreign land. As you step off the bus, the local people crowd towards you, gesticulating and shouting. Their words sound like animal cries. Their gestures mean nothing to you. Your first instinct might be to fight, to push these intruders away from you; to fly, to run away from their incomprehensible demands; or to freeze, to try to ignore the chaos around you.

The world of the person with autism may be rather like this. If autistic people lack the ability to "think about thoughts", their own as well as others', then they are like strangers in a foreign land, because the world we inhabit is a social world. The most important element in our surroundings is human. We make sense of behaviour in terms of mental states. Without such a "theory of mind", the social world must be a terrifying, unpredictable place. No wonder the autistic child often fights against it, or withdraws from it physically or mentally.

What is the practical value of this insight? Much of the autistic person's strange behaviour can be better understood if we remember that he cannot "mind-read" in the way most of us do. Take for example the autistic girl who had a tantrum every time she was told she was going swimming, until someone thought to say, "we're going swimming – *and we're coming back*"! Without an understanding of the intentions behind speech, communication breaks down, as for the autistic child who in response to the request, "Can you pass the salt" replies in all earnestness, "Yes". Understanding the autistic child's "mind-blindness" can also help parents, who often have to face apparently unkind behaviour from their children. A child who enjoys making people cry may seem cruel, but without insight into emotions, provoking tears may be as rewarding as and more interesting than prompting a smile.

Unanswered questions

Of course, the mind-blindness theory of autism cannot explain everything, and puzzles still remain in this fascinating disorder. For example, it has been consistently found that a minority of autistic children in any study will pass theory of mind tasks (in Baron-Cohen et al. (1985), 20 per cent of autistic subjects passed). How can a lack of theory of mind explain autism if some, still handicapped, autistic people appear to possess a theory of mind? This question will arise again in Chapter 6, and be discussed at some length in Chapter 7.

There are other unsolved questions. For example, can a "mind-blind-ness" theory of autism explain the non-social handicaps in autism? What theory can shed light on features such as insistence on sameness, stereo-typies, self-injurious behaviour? It is part of the excitement and frustration of research that there are always further questions to ask, and new theories to be developed. Chapter 10 looks to the future and makes some specula-tive suggestions concerning the cognitive cause of the puzzling non-social assets and deficits in autism.

Conclusions

When we try to understand the mind of an individual with autism, we are looking for an explanation of autism at the cognitive level. In this chapter some of the characteristics of a good theory at the cognitive level have been discussed, and one candidate theory reviewed. The idea that autistic peo-ple suffer from a specific impairment in "mind-reading" has been presented at some length, as an example of a cognitive theory which has exceptional explanatory power and specificity. Many puzzles still remain, which will only be answered through making and testing new hypotheses. In the next chapter some other psychological theories are discussed, each of which attempts in its own way to solve the puzzle of autism.

Suggested reading

Baron-Cohen, S. 1993. From attention–goal psychology to belief–desire psychology: the development of a theory of mind, and its dysfunction. In *Understanding other minds: perspectives from autism*, S. Baron-Cohen, H. Tager-Flusberg, D. J. Cohen (eds), 59–82. Oxford: Oxford University Press.

Frith, U., J. Morton, A. M. Leslie 1991. The cognitive basis of a biological disorder: autism. *Trends in Neuroscience* **14**, 433–8.

Happé, F. & U. Frith 1994. Theory of mind in autism. In *Learning and cognition in autism*, E. Schopler & G. B. Mesibov (eds). New York: Plenum Press.

Chapter 6

Autism at the cognitive level: alternatives to theory of mind

Criteria for theories of autism: parsimony and primacy

In the previous chapter a psychological theory of autism was discussed which aimed to explain the triad of impairments in autism in terms of a single underlying cognitive deficit – a failure or delay in mentalizing. A desire for parsimony has been evident in many other theories of autism – with authors postulating the minimum number of underlying psychological impairments necessary to account for the behavioural manifestations of autism. However, more recently, other authors have suggested that autism is likely to be the result of multiple primary deficits, either at the biological (Goodman 1989) or at the psychological level (e.g. Ozonoff et al. 1991a). Clearly, it is possible that deficits which are unconnected at the psychological level may occur together more often than by chance alone, due to the spatial proximity of their biological substrates in the brain (cf. pattern (a) in Figure 1.1). In this case, just as for purely physical markers of disorders (e.g. physiognomy of Down's syndrome), it may be futile to look for a common cause at the psychological level. Such theories of autism, then, are not primarily psychological in nature, and will not be considered here. However, noting this issue should act as a useful reminder of the importance of keeping clear at all times the level (biological, psychological, behavioural) at which one is attempting an explanation (Morton & Frith 1994). A number of recent theories of autism are based primarily at the biological level (e.g. Damasio & Maurer 1978, Panksepp & Shaley 1987, Dawson & Lewy 1989, Dawson 1991) and are reviewed elsewhere (Pennington & Welsh 1994).

Three commonly accepted criteria for assessing the primacy of a deficit are universality among sufferers of the disorder, specificity to the disorder, and causal precedence in the disorder. In addition, as mentioned in

Chapter 5, theories of autism must steer a course between explaining too little – in effect merely describing features – and explaining too much. People with autism show a strikingly uneven profile of abilities, and show islets of unimpaired or even superior skills which require explanation just as much as do the striking handicaps. The challenge then is to propose a psychological deficit significant enough to cause the severe impairments of autism, and specific enough to allow areas of preserved functioning.

The challenge to other theories

In Chapter 5 the theory of mind account of autism was discussed, and the experimental work supporting this hypothesis was reviewed. While other psychological theories of autism should not be seen merely as responses to or criticisms of this theory, each in its way presents an alternative which aims to fill gaps in the theory of mind account. Other psychological theories of autism have responded to this body of work in a number of ways. Current theories of autism can be grouped under the following headings:
- (a) those which claim that failure on false belief tasks (e.g. the Sally–Ann task) does not reflect a lack of mentalizing but rather some other impairment, or task artifact;
- (b) those which accept that failure on false belief tasks reflects a lack of mentalizing, but deny that this is the primary, core psychological impairment on the basis of
  - (i) lack of universality of this deficit,
  - (ii) lack of causal precedence of this deficit.

Does failure on false belief tasks reflect inability to mentalize?

The false belief paradigm was originally proposed as a test safe from false positives (Dennett 1978). However, concern has been expressed about the meaning of task failure, either by subjects with autism or by normally developing young children (e.g. Siegal & Beattie 1991). Clearly, tasks designed to tap the ability to represent mental states also involve other psychological abilities (e.g. language, memory), and an impairment in one of these other areas might lead to task failure which was not a true indication of a mentalizing deficit.

Some researchers have suggested that autistic failure on false belief tasks is an artifact of the task structure; due to pragmatic difficulties with the wording of the test question (Eisenmajer & Prior 1991), grammatical difficulties not tapped by measures used for verbal mental age matching (Boucher 1989), or lack of motivation to deceive (DeGelder 1987). Most such criticisms do not address the finding that children with autism fail a whole array of false belief tasks, with very different controls and methodologies. For example, in a recent study by Sodian & Frith (1992), autistic children's ability to keep a sweet from a puppet competitor by deception and by sabotage was examined (Figure 6.1). By contrasting these two conditions it was possible to rule out lack of motivation or failure to comprehend the instructions. The only difference between the two conditions was that deception (lying or pointing to the empty location) manipulated the competitor's beliefs, while sabotage (locking the box where the sweet was) simply manipulated his behaviour. In each condition, the children also had to refrain from misleading or obstructing a puppet co-operator who helped the child. In this experiment the children with autism proved surprisingly competent at sabotage but largely incapable of deception. Such well designed experiments would appear to render explanations of autistic failure in terms of methodological artifacts untenable.

Russell and his colleagues (Russell et al. 1991, Hughes & Russell 1993) propose an alternative psychological theory of autism, which centres on the child's "*inability to disengage from the object*". Russell suggests that the autistic child's failure on false belief tasks does not reflect a mentalizing deficit, but rather a specific difficulty in overcoming the perceptual salience of the object in the real location. The authors suggest that this same core deficit could account for failure on other mentalizing tasks, such as deception, where the correct answer involves indicating the empty location and suppressing a response to the actual physical location of the hidden object. They tested this hypothesis by examining the effect of a competitor on performance on Russell's "windows task". In this task the child simply had to point to one of two boxes, into which he/she alone could see via a small window. On each trial a sweet was placed in one of the boxes, and if the child indicated the empty box (versus the second, baited box), he won the sweet. In the competitor version, an ignorant second player searched in the indicated box, and kept any sweets thus found – so that the child was effectively rewarded for "deceiving" the competitor. Hughes & Russell (1993) found that autistic subjects were as bad at the "windows" task without a competitor as with – and concluded that their difficulties with deception did not spring from an inability to mentalize, but from a failure to inhibit action to the object. However, the logic behind their conclusion (that if found equally hard, the element of deception itself is not the problem for the autistic subjects) only holds if the two tasks are otherwise equated for difficulty. As it was, the no-opponent task was certainly less natural, and indeed, the mentally handicapped controls in this experiment performed worse on the no-opponent than the opponent task.

Subsequent studies by Hughes (1993), however, have shown that on a number of non-social tasks (e.g. a computer version of the Tower of Hanoi, and a detour reach task) most children with autism do show some impairment when required to act away from the object or to inhibit a prepotent (previously rewarded) response. In this respect, Russell's theory is clearly related to other recent suggestions that autism involves an executive function deficit similar to that seen in adults with acquired frontal lobe lesions (see Ch. 4) (Ozonoff et al. 1991a, see below). However, Russell differs from some other authors in suggesting that a mentalizing deficit need not be invoked in order to explain the body of theory of mind results. Closely controlled studies, such as that by Sodian & Frith (1992), make this argument less compelling. Nor is it clear why a failure to disengage from the object should lead to incorrect response in the "true belief" task of Leslie & Frith (1988), where the child is required to point to one of the actual locations of the object(s). Recent studies by Leekam & Perner (1991), Leslie & Thaiss (1992) and Charman & Baron-Cohen (1992), discussed in Chapter 5, show that children with autism are not impaired at answering questions about a non-current state of the world – as portrayed in a now-out-of-date photograph or drawing. It is not clear, then, what extra demands the standard false belief tasks place upon disengagement from the object. Arguments about the lesser salience of mental representations for autistic children beg the question, and render Russell's theory less distinct from mentalizing-deficit theories in both nature and predictions. The same arguments would appear to apply to Harris's (1993) suggestion that autistic children's false belief task failure is due to executive function problems which result in a deficit in internal versus external control – leading to impairments whenever the current state of reality must be put aside and a contrary, imagined state invoked.

Is the mentalizing deficit the primary, core impairment?

Several authors accept that the autistic subject's failure on false belief tasks does reflect an inability to mentalize, but do not accept that this is the core

Figure 6.1 The sabotage and deception tasks (Sodian & Frith 1992; by kind permission of the artist, Axel Scheffler).

Figure 6.1 The sabotage and deception tasks, continued.

or primary psychological impairment in autism. Alternative theories high-light two apparent weaknesses in the mentalizing-deficit account: not all people with autism fail false belief tasks, and mentalizing deficits may in any case spring from some other, primary impairment.

Is a mentalizing deficit universal in autism?

In every study testing autistic children's performance on mentalizing tasks, some proportion of subjects is found to pass. The percentage of successful children has varied from 15 per cent (Reed & Peterson 1990) to 60 per cent (Prior et al. 1990) of the sample, which is preselected to be sufficiently bright and verbal to attempt standard false belief tasks. In most, but not all, cases the proportion of successful autistic subjects is significantly smaller than the proportion of successful subjects in verbal mental age-matched (normal or mentally handicapped) control groups. However, the finding that *any* child with autism passes false belief tasks has been seen by many as fatally dam-aging to the mentalizing-deficit theory of autism. If an inability to repre-sent the beliefs and desires of others (and self) leads to the triad of behavioural impairments which characterize autism, how can it be that individuals exist who *pass* tests of mentalizing and yet are still autistic?

Bowler (1992) found that a sample of 15 high-functioning autistic adults, who had received the "Asperger's syndrome" label (see Ch. 8), performed well on mentalizing tasks at two levels of difficulty, and were no worse on these tasks than normal controls or schizophrenic adults. Bowler suggests that this success on false belief tests, in the presence of continuing real-life handicaps, argues for a primary psychological deficit not in mentalizing but in *applying existing knowledge*. This idea is similar to Boucher's (1989) sugges-tion that autism is primarily due to a "failure to use available skills", or "to spontaneously use higher order representational systems".

To be more than a description of findings, and to allow testable predic-tions, such a suggestion must explain *why* subjects with autism fail to apply knowledge which they possess. Bowler suggests that the good task perform-ance of his subjects is based on rather different mechanisms from normal mentalizing: "although people with Asperger's syndrome can compute cor-rect solutions to problems requiring a theory of mind, they do so by routes that are slow and cumbersome, disrupting the timing of their responses and making them appear odd in everyday social interactions". Elsewhere he talks of their ability to "circumvent their lack of intuitive knowledge of social behaviour to a sufficient degree to pass . . . problems . . . in test situations but not in real-life".

Although Bowler sees his results as damaging to the mentalizing-deficit account of autism, his theory is similar to the explanation of task success given by Frith et al. (1991) who propose this account. They argue that although some people with autism do pass false belief tasks, they do not in fact have the ability to mentalize. Rather, they suggest, these subjects have found a task-specific strategy which allows them to "hack out" a solution to these artificial tests, but which does not (unlike true mentalizing) generalize to real-life social situations. One prediction might be, for example, that although quite a number of subjects with autism pass the Sally–Ann task, many fewer would actually perform consistently well if tested with a whole range of different false belief tasks. Indeed, Happé (1994a) found that even a group of autistic subjects who passed standard second-order theory of mind tasks made errors in a more advanced test where they were required to explain a speaker's motivation in cases of double bluff, persuasion and misunderstanding (see Ch. 7).

In general, however, researchers have equated the passing of false belief tasks with the possession of mentalizing competence. Ozonoff et al. (1991a) tested 23 children with autism and average IQ on batteries of theory of mind, executive function and emotion perception tasks, in order to explore the "primary configuration of deficits". *Executive function* is defined as the ability to maintain an appropriate problem-solving set for attainment of a future goal, and is associated with the frontal lobes (for a review, see Duncan 1986). To assess executive function Ozonoff et al. used two tasks. In the Wisconsin Card Sorting Test (WCST) the subject is required to deduce a (periodically changed) rule for sorting cards by either colour, shape or number, using feedback from the examiner about the correctness of each sort. In the Tower of Hanoi task, the subject must reproduce a configuration of discs on three pegs, keeping to certain rules which in effect require the subject to plan moves in advance and inhibit prepotent but inappropriate responses.

Compared to age- and verbal IQ-matched controls, the subjects with autism showed impairments in each of the three areas tested: executive functions, emotion recognition, and theory of mind. The authors found that executive function and theory of mind deficits were significantly more widespread among the autistic subjects than other deficits (for a review of this study, and of possible relations between executive function and theory of mind deficits in autism, see Bishop 1993). In an accompanying study, Ozonoff et al. (1991b) found that problems with mentalizing tasks at two

levels of difficulty were restricted to their "high-functioning autistic" subjects and were not found in a group they labelled as having "Asperger's
syndrome" (but see Ch. 8 for problems with differentiating this diagnosis).
By contrast, the Asperger's syndrome subjects, like the other autistic subjects
in their sample, did show executive function deficits; they were less efficient
on the Tower of Hanoi test, and were more perseverative (failing to shift
from an old sorting rule) on the WCST. On the basis that Asperger's syndrome is currently believed to be a subtype of autism, with the same
underlying psychological deficit, Ozonoff et al. argue that executive function deficits are a better candidate than mentalizing deficits for the core and
primary impairment in autism. However, these authors do not discard the
mentalizing-deficit explanation for much of the triad of impairments in
many children with autism. They discuss possible connections between
these two psychological deficits. Executive function deficits may be the result
of mentalizing problems, mentalizing problems may result from executive
function deficits, or both may result from a third factor. Based on their finding that some individuals with autism exist (those labelled as having
Asperger's syndrome) who have executive function problems but no
mentalizing deficit, the authors conclude that some third deficit must be
responsible for the two measured impairments in most subjects with autism.
Surprisingly, they postulate a third factor not at the psychological level but
at the biological level: damage to the prefrontal cortex.

Chapter 7 considers in some detail the nature of the underlying competence in those autistic subjects who pass theory of mind tasks. A couple
of points should be made here, however, concerning the finding that some
subjects with autism do pass false belief tasks. First, it is as well to remember that any task is at best a distant probe to underlying competence: there
may be as many ways to pass a test as there are to fail it. It remains to be
seen whether yet harder mentalizing tasks would, in fact, reveal autism-
specific deficits which would be universal to this population (Happé 1994a),
or, indeed, whether apparently good performance would break down across
different examples of mentalizing tasks.

Even if some people with autism *can* think about thoughts, this does not
rule out a causal rôle for mentalizing problems in autistic *development*. A *delay
hypothesis* (Baron-Cohen 1989b) is still tenable – there has not been reported
to date an autistic child of verbal mental age 4 years who passes false belief
tasks. It is easy to forget the importance of development when considering
primary deficits in autism. So, although there may be evidence of
mentalizing ability now, this does not necessarily mean that the ability was

present at earlier (possibly critical) points in development. Similarly, although the pattern found by Ozonoff et al. suggests that mentalizing problems do not cause executive function problems (or vice versa) *on-line* (in processing time), these data cannot tell us whether either of these deficits played a causal rôle in the other *developmentally* (cf. Ch. 1).

Is a mentalizing deficit primary or secondary?

Several authors have felt that to define the core impairment in a disorder as severe as autism in terms of a process as apparently sophisticated as metarepresentation or mentalizing is to underestimate the very basic nature of the autistic breakdown of social ability. Many theorists, then, while not denying that the child with autism may have difficulties in mentalizing, suggest a more basic primary impairment which may or may not give rise later in development to an inability to think about thoughts.

Hobson (1989, 1990, 1993a,b) has maintained that the mentalizing deficit is but one sequel of a much deeper impairment which prevents the child from establishing normal *interpersonal relatedness* with those around him. This author views autism as primarily an affective and interpersonal impairment, which cannot be defined without regard to the child's relationship to care-givers. Disruptions to the early processes of joint attention, and particularly of the "triangulation" of attention and emotion involving baby, adult and object, are postulated to occur in autism due to innate brain abnormalities. Hobson postulates an innate impairment in the ability to perceive and respond to the affective expressions of others, and suggests that due to this deficit children with autism do not receive the necessary social experiences in infancy and childhood to develop the cognitive structures for social understanding.

Hobson's theoretical perspective has led him to study emotion perception deficits in autism (Hobson 1986a,b, Hobson et al. 1989). Work in this area has recently been critically reviewed by Ozonoff et al. (1990), who point out that significant deficits only emerge relative to controls matched on *non-verbal* IQ. The uneven IQ profile and superior non-verbal or performance scores of most subjects with autism make such matching procedures problematic. However, the recent work of Ozonoff et al. with high-functioning autistic subjects has found emotion perception impairments even relative to a control group matched for age and verbal IQ (Ozonoff et al. 1991). Some of Hobson's most interesting work, perhaps, is that which suggests that regardless of *level* of performance on emotion recognition tasks, individuals with autism appear to go about such tasks very differently from control subjects – as reflected, for example, in the lesser disruption they experience from an inverted presentation of faces (Langdell 1978, Hobson et al. 1988).

To date Hobson's theory has been hard either to prove or disprove – since the crux of the matter lies in causal priorities. Most symptoms of autism (e.g. failure to recognize emotional expressions) could, in themselves, be explained by a primary deficit in either mentalizing or interpersonal relatedness – and can be seen as either springing directly from such a deficit or developing as a secondary consequence.

An attempt has been made to establish causal priority for emotional deficits by suggesting that children with autism show behavioural abnormalities before the age at which metarepresentational abilities emerge in normal children. Mundy & Sigman (1989) have argued that the fact that children with autism do not show *joint attention behaviours*, which develop prior to pretence in the normal child, proves that autism results from a deficit other than (and earlier than) an inability to metarepresent. However, this argument rests on the assumption that the emergence of pretence marks the emergence of metarepresentation. This, as Leslie & Happé (1989) have argued, is unlikely. While pretence is an early sign that metarepresentations must be available to the child, even earlier ostensive communication behaviours such as joint attention may also signal the emergence of the ability to represent mental states, since these behaviours convey the intention to communicate. However, this does not invalidate Mundy et al.'s (1993) point that joint attention involves an affective component, the capacity to share and compare one's own and others' emotional expressions *vis-à-vis* a third referent. Their argument about primacy, then, is in part an argument about the failure of theory of mind accounts of autism to consider the affective aspects of representing mental states (Sigman et al. 1992, Yirmiya et al. 1992).

Very recently Baron-Cohen (1994) has suggested that mentalizing deficits may be secondary to an earlier emerging impairment in the capacity to build "triadic representations". Within the visual modality he postulates an *eye direction detector* which develops early in normal infants and feeds information to a *shared attention mechanism*. This mechanism normally builds triadic representations of self–other–object relations (enabling joint attention), but which is deficient in children with autism. He suggests that disruption to such a mechanism might significantly disturb the child's social development and awareness of other people as goal-directed beings capable of attending to objects. Phillips et al. (1992) have demonstrated that, unlike normally developing 9 to 18-month-olds, children with autism (aged 3 years 4 months to 7 years 2 months) did not use eye contact as a source of information in a naturalistic situation where an adult's goal was ambiguous.

A persuasive argument for *prementalizing deficits* in autism is made by Klin et al. (1992). These authors focused on social behaviours which normally develop before the age at which even the earliest signs of metarepresentation or mentalizing are shown. As these authors point out, much of the merit of the mentalizing deficit account of autism lies in its specificity – the prediction that discrete impairments will be seen, affecting only those behaviours which require the representation of mental states. Klin et al. used the first 20 items of the Socialization domain of the Vineland Adaptive Behavior Scales (Sparrow et al. 1984) to assess the social competence of 29 young autistic children (mean age 4.3 years, mean mental age 1.8 years). Most of the 20 items detailed behaviours expected in normal development by age 8 months. Compared with a chronological and mental age matched control group, significantly fewer of the children with autism were reported by their care-givers as regularly showing nine of the 20 early social behaviours. The authors conclude that "in contrast to predictions derived from the Theory of Mind hypothesis, social deficits in autism include very basic and early emerging socially adaptive behaviours . . . ". Indeed it would be hard to argue that behaviours such as "shows anticipation of being picked up by care-giver" or "reaches for familiar person" necessitate mentalizing ability.

Klin et al. point out, however, that there were *some* autistic subjects among their sample who did show many or most of these early social behaviours. They suggest that this may indicate the existence of subgroups, with different pathogenic pathways. In addition, the very early recognition of autism in the subjects of Klin et al. is not typical of the whole spectrum of autistic children – those with higher ability are often not diagnosed until much later, and indeed those studied by Klin et al. were all developmentally delayed. It remains an open question, then, whether more able autistic children would show the same primary social impairments, and whether the very social abnormalities Klin et al. measured played a part in the early identification (and hence selection) of the sample studied. It may be, for example, that their sample consisted of those children who are "aloof" in Wing's characterization (Wing & Attwood 1987), and are not representative in this respect of those other autistic children who would be described as "passive" or "active but odd".

Rogers & Pennington (1991) have also suggested that earlier social-cognitive deficits may be primary in autism and result in mentalizing deficits as well as emotion recognition problems. They suggest that infants with autism may have deficits in *imitation* and emotion sharing which affect the child's ability to "organize *social* information by depriving the baby of primary sources of social data – mother–baby imitations and amodal perception of emotion via the mother's bodily expression". As development continues, it is hypothesized, these core deficits disrupt the autistic infant's ability to share affect with care-givers, which in turn affects the social representations the infant builds up, and his/her ability to develop a theory of mind.

The rôle of normal infant imitation in social development is also discussed by Meltzoff & Gopnik (1993). They suggest that mutual imitation is effectively a "tutorial in early common-sense psychology". The ability of new born babies to imitate a seen facial expression leads the authors to postulate an innate supramodal (i.e. modality independent) body schema, allowing matching of seen (visual) information with felt (proprioceptive) information. The authors speculate that imitation may in fact be the origins of "emotional contagion" – that by assuming the same facial expression as those around him, the infant may come to experience the same emotions. In the case of autism, Meltzoff & Gopnik suggest that this innate system of imitation, which they claim allows the baby to identify the adult as "something like me", is defective. This lack of the "initial starting-state", in their words, would limit the evidence available to the child for the construction of a representational theory of mind. This hypothesis raises many interesting questions: *Are* autistic children impaired in basic emotional contagion? Will there be other groups who, for different reasons (e.g. blindness, paralysis, parental neglect), also have limits placed on their ability to engage in mutual imitation, and hence in the evidence they gather for understanding minds? Would Meltzoff & Gopnik predict a social impairment, qualitatively similar to autism, in these groups also? Preliminary evidence about the development of pretend play, at least, seems to go against such an idea; for example, comprehension of pretence develops normally (if with a delay) in many blind children (Rogers & Pulchalski 1984).

Perner (1993) has also suggested that the autistic child's lack of ability to mentalize may result from an early deficit which disrupts the child's ability to amass normal social experience. Perner's own view of normal development leads him to hypothesize that the child with autism fails to develop a representational theory of mind. This, he suggests, is due to some basic biologically-caused disorder, such as an inability to shift attention rapidly, which in turn disrupts the relevant experiences and database necessary for the normal development of a concept of representation.

Primary deficits and early indicators of autism

Theories which grant mentalizing deficits a rôle in autism, but which argue for the existence of earlier core deficits, face a number of challenges. Autism is currently diagnosed only in toddlerhood, but researchers are increasingly interested in the autistic infant. Assumptions are often made, therefore, about *developmental continuities*. While it is certainly striking to find that autistic 4-year-olds do not show behaviours which normal 8-month-olds display, this does not necessarily tell us about the competence which the autistic child possesses or lacks in early infancy. So, for example, many parents claim that their autistic child did show social interest and even developed some words early in development, but lost these skills at around the second birthday. If these reports were confirmed, it might suggest that early emerging social and communicative behaviours rely upon mechanisms which are different from, and superseded by, those underlying later competence in these areas. This argument is particularly relevant for the consideration of imitation deficits, where it seems likely that neonatal imitation may be subserved by a mechanism separate from that underlying later childhood imitation. Indeed, Lord (1991) claims that a significant minority of parents report evidence of imitation during the infancy of autistic children who are later found to be incapable of reproducing a modelled action on demand.

As described in Chapter 3, recent studies suggest that it is not until the second year of life that autism-specific social abnormalities are generally recognized. If it were confirmed that autism is not detectable (in at least some subjects) before the second year, this would have clear implications for many theories of autism which postulate basic deficits in very early emerging social abilities in all children with autism.

Conclusions

Recent psychological theories of autism have focused on the social impairment as the key feature of autism. In this respect all the theories discussed in this chapter, as well as the mentalizing-deficit theory discussed in Chapter

5, are alike – each postulates a core psychological deficit which results in the triad of handicaps in communication, socialization and imagination. The process of refining and debating notions of the autistic social impairment, which is reflected in these two chapters, has perhaps led us to neglect other features of autism. In Chapter 10, we return to this question, and look at a different sort of psychological theory of autism, which seeks to explain both the (non-social) handicaps and skills of individuals with autism.

Suggested reading

Bishop, D. V. M. 1993. Annotation: autism, executive functions and theory of mind: a neuropsychological perspective. *Journal of Child Psychology and Psychiatry* **34**, 279–94.

Hobson, R. P. 1993. Understanding persons: the rôle of affect. In *Understanding other minds: perspectives from autism*, S. Baron-Cohen, H. Tager-Flusberg, D. J. Cohen (eds), 204–27. Oxford: Oxford University Press.

Rutter, M. & A. Bailey 1993. Thinking and relationships: mind and brain (some reflections on theory of mind and autism). In *Understanding other minds: perspectives from autism*, S. Baron-Cohen, H. Tager-Flusberg, D. J. Cohen (eds), 481–504. Oxford: Oxford University Press.

Chapter 7

The talented minority

Chapter 5 described a recent and influential cognitive explanation of the triad of social, communication and imagination impairments found in autism. This theory suggests that autistic people lack a theory of mind, and are not able to attribute independent mental states (such as false beliefs) to themselves and others. As Chapter 5 showed, this theory has been quite successful in explaining the pattern of impaired and preserved functioning in many people with autism. Chapter 6 reviewed some other psychological theories of autism, and looked at some of the major criticisms of the theory of mind approach. In particular, the issue of primacy was discussed at some length. Here, we look again at the question of universality: do all people with autism suffer from "mind-blindness"?

Explaining theory of mind test success

In every study using theory of mind tests, some people with autism are found to pass. How can we explain this test success? The first question is whether those autistic subjects who pass theory of mind tests are actually capable of representing mental states – does mentalizing underlie their test success? If not, then an inability to mentalize may still be universal to autism. If, on the other hand, we believe that some autistic people can represent mental states, we are faced with the puzzle of their continued social and communicative handicaps. To explain these we might hypothesize either a damaging delay in acquisition, or a persisting additional impairment which hampers use of mentalizing in everyday life. In this chapter some possible explanations of task success are examined, and some empirical evidence from very recent studies is discussed. The nature of social ability in the most able individuals with autism has been the focus of my own research to date, and so much of the work discussed here is mine, and some of the theoretical analyses reflect my own personal perspective.

The strategy hypothesis

One way of explaining the success of a minority of autistic people on false belief tasks is to suggest that they pass these tests using a non-theory of mind strategy. Some autistic people may have managed to "hack out" a solution to theory of mind tasks thanks to experience, using general problem-solving skills (Frith et al. 1991). Such "hacking" may be relatively inflexible, allowing success only on very artificial, simplified "mind-reading" tests, such as are typically given in theory of mind experiments. In real life these strategies may not be very useful, leaving the person socially handicapped in spite of their good test performance.

To date there has been no exploration of the non-mentalizing strategies which might underlie false belief task success. One possible strategy might be to associate person–object–place; for example, in the Sally–Ann task, Sally–marble–basket. This strategy would allow the child to pass the Sally–Ann task without representing mental states, but would not generalize to other theory of mind tests such as the Smarties task, or to real life "mentalizing" skills such as keeping secrets. One way to assess non-theory of mind strategies, then, might be to look at real-life behaviour which seems to require insight into other minds. Another might be to look for inconsistencies across batteries of different false belief tasks. A third approach might be to look at the relationship between test success and general intellectual ability or age – presumably developing a strategy requires some amount of reasoning ability and experience. By contrast, in normal development a mental age of 5 years is sufficient to pass standard theory of mind tests, and to demonstrate this ability across a range of different tasks (Gopnik & Astington 1988). Mentally handicapped subjects, too, pass these tasks with relatively impaired general intellectual and problem-solving abilities (Baron-Cohen et al. 1985).

Real mentalizing: the delay hypothesis

It may be that autistic people are merely grossly delayed in their acquisition of a theory of mind, and that it is therefore no surprise that a few autistic people should manage to pass these tests eventually. Baron-Cohen

(1989b) found that while some autistic subjects passed the Sally–Ann task, none of these subjects passed a harder, "second-order" theory of mind task: the ice-cream van task (adapted from Perner & Wimmer 1985). In this task, the subject is shown a village scene with a park, church and houses. The subject is introduced to John and Mary figures, and shown that they are in the park. The following story is told as the figures act out the events:

> This is Mary and this is John. Today they are in the park. Along comes the ice cream van. John wants to buy an ice cream, but he has left his money at home. He'll have to go home first and get his money before he can buy an ice cream. The ice cream man tells John, "It's alright John, I'll be here in the park all day. So you can go and get your money and come back and buy your ice cream. I'll still be here." So John runs off home to get his money.
>
> But, when John has gone, the ice cream man changes his mind. He decides he won't stay in the park all afternoon, instead he'll go and sell ice cream outside the church. He tells Mary, "I won't stay in the park, like I said. I'm going to the church instead".

Comprehension check 1: Did John hear the ice cream man tell Mary that?

> So in the afternoon, Mary goes home and the ice cream man sets off for the church. But on his way he meets John. So he tells John, "I changed my mind, I won't be in the park, I'm going to sell ice cream outside the church this afternoon". The ice cream man then drives to the church.

Comprehension check 2: Did Mary hear the ice cream man tell John that?

> In the afternoon, Mary goes over to John's house and knocks on the door. John's mother answers the door and says, "Oh, I'm sorry Mary, John's gone out. He's gone to buy an ice cream".

Belief question: Where does Mary think John has gone to buy an ice cream?

Justification question: Why does Mary think that?

Reality question: Where did John really go to buy his ice cream?

Memory question: Where was the ice cream van in the beginning?

This task tests the child's ability to represent one character's (false) *belief* about what another character *thinks* about the world: Mary *thinks* John doesn't *know* that the ice cream van is at the church. It is therefore referred to as a "second-order" task, since it requires one more level of embedding than do "first-order" false belief tasks such as the Sally–Ann test, where the child need only represent Sally's (false) *belief* about the world. Normal children pass second-order false belief tasks between 5 and 7 years of age (Perner & Wimmer 1985).

Baron-Cohen found that all of his sample of 10 subjects with autism failed this harder theory of mind task, and suggested that even those subjects who pass the Sally–Ann task show significantly delayed understanding of minds (all his subjects were well over 7 years old, with an expressive verbal mental age (VMA) of 7 to 17 years). However, other studies have found that more able subjects with autism – those sometimes described as having Asperger's syndrome – are able to pass even second-order theory of mind tasks. As Chapter 6 described, both Bowler (1992) and Ozonoff et al. (1991b) have demonstrated good performance on these tasks, and have suggested that this crucially undermines the claim that a theory of mind deficit is the core cognitive impairment in autism.

The finding that some people with autism can pass theory of mind tasks to a 7-year-old level does not, however, rule out two remaining interpretations of a delay hypothesis. First, it is possible that even subjects who pass second-order theory of mind tasks may fail still more advanced tests of mentalizing. Secondly, even subjects who at the age of testing (usually in their teens or later) consistently pass theory of mind tasks may not have acquired this competence at the normal age. That is, a significant delay in developing the ability to form metarepresentations (to represent mental states) may be universal to autism, even if a persisting inability to mentalize is not. Delay may itself have damaging consequences, for example disrupting the normal interaction of this system with other areas of development, and, at the very least, robbing the individual of years of formative social experience. The only way to disprove this developmental delay hypothesis for autism, then, is to find a clearly autistic child who passes all available tests of theory of mind *at the normal age* (or mental age). No such child has yet been found.

Looking for evidence: assessing "true" theory of mind

Three strands of evidence, then, may give clues to the real nature of autistic theory of mind task success; the relation between task success and other subject characteristics, the relation between task success in the laboratory and mentalizing ability in real life, and the generalization of success across different theory of mind tasks.

Task success, age and intelligence

In several studies of autistic theory of mind some analysis of the rôle of age and mental age in task performance has been attempted. Not surprisingly, in view of the relatively small sample sizes, different authors have come to different conclusions. Some have found little relation between theory of mind task performance and subject characteristics (Baron-Cohen et al. 1985, Perner et al. 1989). Others have found a relationship with *chronological age* (CA), with older autistic subjects being more likely to pass (Leslie & Frith 1988, Baron-Cohen 1991). So, for example, in Baron-Cohen's (1992) study the four autistic subjects who passed the false belief task were all older than 9.9 years, and three of the four were older than 15 years. He concluded that a relatively high age was necessary but not sufficient for autistic subjects to pass the Smarties task. Still other authors (e.g. Eisenmajer & Prior 1991) have found a relationship between theory of mind task success and *verbal mental age* (VMA). In Leekam & Perner's (1991) sample, the VMA of the six subjects who passed was significantly higher than that of the failers (7 years 5 months versus 6 years), and the correlation between VMA and task success was significantly greater than zero ($r = .49$). Prior et al. (1990) concluded that both VMA and CA play a rôle in task success; among the nine autistic subjects in their sample with a VMA below 6 years 3 months only 11 per cent passed all the tasks, while 64 per cent of the autistic subjects with a VMA over 6 years 3 months passed all three tasks. In addition, none of the seven autistic children in their sample aged below 8 years passed all tasks, while 62% of the 13 autistic children aged 8 years or older passed.

In the search for relationships between theory of mind task performance and subject characteristics, studies of autistic individuals have been hampered by small sample sizes. Recently, I have tried to overcome this problem by collating the data collected over 5 years by members of the MRC Cognitive Development Unit, from a large sample of subjects tested in a standard fashion on the same tasks (Happé 1994c). The group of subjects with autism was not only large but also diverse, covering a wide range of ages and ability levels. For each subject information on age, verbal mental age and verbal IQ (from the British Picture Vocabulary Scale) was collated, as well as the subject's performance on the Sally–Ann and Smarties tasks.

Complete data were available for 70 normal 3- and 4-year-olds, 34 mentally handicapped children, and 70 autistic children. The groups of individuals with autism and of subjects with mental handicap were of very similar age (from 6 to 18 years old, mean age 12 years), VMA (mean 6 years) and verbal IQ (mean around 55).

In this large group, as in previous smaller samples, only a minority (20 per cent) of children with autism succeeded on theory of mind tasks, while a greater proportion (58 per cent) of non-autistic mentally handicapped subjects passed these tasks. In addition, in the autistic group there was a strong and significant relationship between theory of mind task success and verbal ability (a correlation of .55). In the mentally handicapped group, subjects who passed and those who failed false belief tasks did not differ in verbal IQ or mental age. However, in the autistic group there was a significant difference; autistic subjects who passed both theory of mind tasks had a mean VMA over 9 years, while those who failed one or both tasks had a mean age of 5.5 years.

Figure 7.1 shows the predicted probability (from logistic regression) of passing both false belief tasks at each VMA. It illustrates graphically the dramatic delay in theory of mind task success shown by the autistic group: while normally developing children had a 50% probability of passing both tasks at the verbal mental age of 4 years, autistic subjects took more than

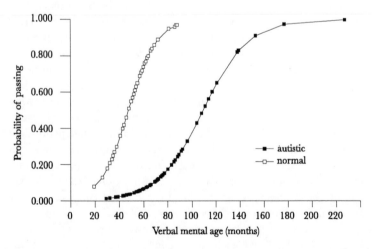

Figure 7.1 Graph showing the predicted probability of passing theory of mind tasks by VMA, for normal young children and individuals with autism (from Happé 1994c)

twice as long to reach this probability of success, having a 50% chance of passing both tasks only at the advanced verbal mental age of 9.2 years.

Figure 7.1 also illustrates the rapid change in theory of mind task performance shown by the young normally developing children; at 3.5 years the predicted probability of passing was .33, at 4.5 years it had almost doubled to .63, and at 5.5 years the probability of success was .80.

Why should autistic subjects require so much greater verbal ability to solve theory of mind tasks than do normally developing children? It seems unlikely that autistic children who fail the Smarties or Sally–Ann tasks do so due to lack of verbal ability in any simple sense; these subjects have VMAs in excess of young normal children who pass, subjects who fail (equally complex) memory and reality control questions are excluded from these tests, and children with specific language impairments do not have special difficulties with false belief tasks (Leslie & Frith 1988).

It is possible that some third factor may underlie both the better verbal ability and the better theory of mind task performance of some autistic subjects. One possibility might be that this successful group is of different aetiology, perhaps more closely approximating what has been called "Asperger's syndrome" (see Ch. 8). VMA, as measured in this study, may be acting as a measure of general ability – and the close relationship it shows to theory of mind task performance may be mediated by overall mental level. This is impossible to rule out in the absence of data on these subjects' performance and full-scale IQ or mental age. However, previous studies, though hampered by small sample sizes, have found no evidence of a relationship between performance on theory of mind tasks and measures of non-verbal ability (Raven's Progressive Matrices test, Charman & Baron-Cohen 1992; Weschler Intelligence Scale for Children – Revised (WISC–R) and Weschler Adult Intelligence Scales (WAIS), Happé 1993). A link between task success and general intellectual ability, if discovered, would seem to support a strategy hypothesis. By contrast, a specific link between theory of mind task performance and verbal ability may suggest that understanding of minds and understanding of language are intimately linked – through the recognition of communicative intent, and perhaps the use by able autistic individuals of verbally-mediated representations of mental states.

Reading minds in everyday life

While the theory of mind deficit hypothesis seems to provide a good theoretical explanation for the pattern of handicaps and abilities seen in autism

(Frith 1989a), the actual link to daily life social impairment has not been tested. One prediction from the hypothesis would be that performance on false belief tasks should relate closely to level of everyday social competence. In particular, if there are autistic subjects who succeed on false belief tasks because they have gained the ability to attribute mental states, they might be expected to show superior levels of social adaptation. A very recent study by Frith et al. (1994) attempted to address this question. These authors measured real-life social behaviour with the Vineland Adaptive Behavior Scales (VABS) (Sparrow et al. 1984), which contain questions for carers about a child's socialization, communication, and daily living skills, as well as maladaptive behaviour. As discussed in Chapter 5, social and communicative behaviour is not all of one type – some but not all such behaviour requires the ability to think about thoughts. Frith et al. devised sets of questions to look more closely at social and communicative behaviours which do or do not require mentalizing. Items were divided into two categories: social behaviours which can be performed without true understanding of mental states (Active), and behaviours which seem to require the attribution of independent mental states (Interactive). So, for example, a child may learn to recognize and label happiness (on the basis of turned-up mouth, etc.) without necessarily being able to mentalize. By contrast, recognition of surprise requires some appreciation of other minds (and particularly the possibility for mistaken beliefs and expectations).

Social behaviour, however, includes unpleasant as well as considerate acts. To capture this dimension of everyday life, Frith et al. categorized selected items from the Maladaptive Behaviour domain of the VABS to form two sets. The Antisocial items covered behaviours, from physical aggression to lying, which made the individual difficult to manage. Some but not all of these behaviours appeared to implicate an awareness of other minds (e.g. lying and cheating). The Bizarre items, on the other hand, consisted entirely of behaviours which seemed to have no relation to mental state understanding (e.g. rocking), and which appeared to be rather typical of autistic individuals at all ability levels. If some subjects with autism can mentalize, then they should show this ability in their greater competence in real-life mentalizing behaviours. That is, they should be more skilled at precisely (and only) those behaviours (nice and nasty) which require mentalizing.

Fifteen young normals, 11 learning disabled, and 24 autistic subjects were tested with the Sally–Ann and Smarties tasks. The groups were chosen to contain some subjects who passed both tasks and some who failed; eight "passers" and 16 "failers" in the autistic group, nine passers and six failers among the young normal children, and six passers and five failers with learning disability. The results showed that, as a group, autistic subjects who passed false belief tasks were significantly better than those who failed on those social behaviours which appear to require a theory of mind (the Interactive items). This social advantage was not general, however, and "passers" were no different from "failers" on the other VABS measures, or on the Active (i.e. non-mentalizing) items. An example of this contrast is shown in Figure 7.2. Interestingly, the autistic subjects who passed the false belief tasks also showed more Antisocial problem behaviours (such as lying and cheating). Frith et al. concluded that some autistic children who consistently pass theory of mind tasks show evidence of mentalizing outside the

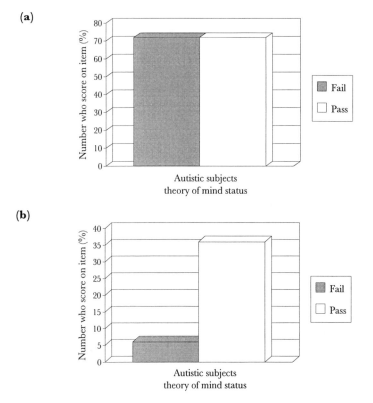

Figure 7.2 Percentages of autistic subjects rated as showing recognition of (a) happiness and sadness ("Active" item) and (b) embarrassment and surprise ("Interactive" item) (from Frith et al. 1994).

laboratory in their everyday lives. It is important to note, however, that even these subjects did not achieve ratings for social adaptation in line with their age or mental age – suggesting perhaps that mentalizing is limited due to late acquisition or additional impairments. In addition, Frith et al.'s results also supported the existence of subgroups within the autistic spectrum – some of whom have no understanding of other minds, some of whom learn limited strategies sufficient to pass highly structured artificial tests of theory of mind, and a small minority of whom are able to represent mental states.

Demonstrating theory of mind across domains; understanding minds in communication

If some autistic people really gain the ability to think about thoughts, albeit with a delay, then we should expect them to show this ability across a wide range of tests. The ability to mentalize is used not only for predicting how a person will behave, or what a person wants or thinks, but also for understanding what a person *means*. In order to understand normal human communication it is vital to look beyond a speaker's words to their intended meaning (Happé 1991a, 1993).

The rôle of understanding mental states in normal human communication has been made particularly clear by Sperber & Wilson's (1986) "relevance theory". One of the important points which these authors make is that communication and language are quite different and separable things. In particular, we can communicate without using language, for example with gestures. Words and sentences are just one type of evidence which we can give to show our intentions. While these tools of communication may make use of agreed meanings, communication is much more than simply encoding and decoding messages (as Morse code operators do). Think about the following example: you ask me how I am feeling after I have just got out of hospital, and in reply I do three cartwheels and a back-flip. There is no code to tell you that I mean by this that I am feeling a lot better – but I have given you good evidence, by my intentional behaviour, that this is what I meant to communicate. So actions can speak as loud as words, because they too can act as clues to our intended meaning. Acts such as these (e.g. pointing, showing, miming) are often described as "ostensive" behaviour – behaviour which makes manifest the intention to communicate. To recognize and engage in ostensive (i.e. communicative) behaviour it is vital to have some recognition of mental states such as intentions.

Communication, then, is another domain where theory of mind skills or deficits should be manifest. Much of my own research has explored the understanding of speakers' intentions in autism, trying to relate this understanding of minds in communication to the understanding of minds in action (e.g. false belief tasks).

To do this I designed a set of stories which concerned the different motivations that can lie behind everyday utterances which are not literally true (Happé 1994a). So, for example, if someone asks your opinion of a new dress which you actually think is hideous, you might say it was nice for a variety of different reasons: to spare their feelings, to mislead them into wearing it and looking awful, to be sarcastic, or to be funny. In everyday life these different motivations will be distinguished by many factors, such as preceding context, emotional expression, and relationship between speaker and hearer. The stories used were written to be largely unambiguous, so that only one interpretation of the situation would be made by normal and non-autistic mentally handicapped subjects. There were two examples of each of 12 story types (see examples in Fig. 7.3): Lie, White Lie, Joke, Pretend, Misunderstanding, Persuade, Appearance/Reality, Figure of Speech, Irony, Forget, Double Bluff and Contrary Emotions. In each story a character says something which is not literally true, and the subject is asked to explain why the character said what he or she did. The prediction was that autistic subjects would have greater difficulty with the stories than the controls, and that autistic subjects' performance would show a strong relation to their performance on the standard theory of mind tasks.

A group of able autistic children and adults were first tested with a battery of standard theory of mind tasks. False belief and deception tasks were given at two levels of complexity: first-order mental states (e.g. "Where does she think the marble is?") and second-order mental states (e.g. "Where does she think John thinks the marble is?"). Performance on the battery was used to select subjects to form three groups: a "no theory of mind" group of six autistic subjects who failed all the theory of mind tasks; a "first-order theory of mind" group of six subjects who performed consistently well at first-order tasks but failed second-order tasks; and a "second-order theory of mind" group of six subjects who performed consistently well at both first- and second-order tasks. Subjects who performed inconsistently were excluded, since inconsistent performance was taken to indicate use of non-mentalizing strategies.

Controls for the experiment were 13 children and adults with moderate learning difficulties (MLD) aged from 12 to 38 years, 26 normal children aged from 6 to 9 years, and 10 normal adults aged from 15 to 24 years. All

Story type: Irony
Ann's mother has spent a long time cooking Ann's favourite meal; fish and chips. But when she brings it in to Ann, she is watching TV, and she doesn't even look up, or say thank you. Ann's mother is cross and says, "Well that's very nice, isn't it! That's what I call politeness!"

Is it true, what Ann's mother says?

Why does Ann's mother say this?

Story type: White Lie
Helen waited all year for Christmas because she knew at Christmas she could ask her parents for a rabbit. Helen wanted a rabbit more than anything in the world. At last Christmas Day arrived, and Helen ran to unwrap the big box her parents had given her. She felt sure it would contain a little rabbit in a cage. But when she opened it, with all the family standing round, she found her present was just a boring old set of encyclopaedias, which Helen did not want at all! Still, when Helen's parents asked her how she liked her present, she said, "It's lovely, thank you. It's just what I wanted".

Is it true what Helen said?

Why did she say that to her parents?

Story type: Lie
One day, while she is playing in the house, Anna accidentally knocks over and breaks her mother's favourite crystal vase. Oh dear, when mother finds out she will be very cross! So when Anna's mother comes home and sees the broken vase and asks Anna what happened, Anna says, "The dog knocked it over, it wasn't my fault!"

Was it true, what Anna told her mother?

Why did she say this?

Story type: Double Bluff

During the war, the Red army capture a member of the Blue army. They want him to tell them where his army's tanks are; they know they are either by the sea or in the mountains. They know that the prisoner will not want to tell them, he will want to save his army, and so he will certainly lie to them. The prisoner is very brave and very clever, he will not let them find his tanks. The tanks are really in the mountains. Now when the other side ask him where his tanks are, he says, "They are in the mountains".

Is it true what the prisoner said?

Where will the other army look for his tanks?

Why did the prisoner say what he said?

Story type: Persuasion

Jane wanted to buy a kitten, so she went to see Mrs. Smith, who had lots of kittens she didn't want. Now Mrs. Smith loved the kittens, and she wouldn't do anything to harm them, though she couldn't keep them all herself. When Jane visited she wasn't sure she wanted one of Mrs. Smith's kittens, since they were all males and she had wanted a female. But Mrs. Smith said, "If no one buys the kittens I'll just have to drown them!"

Was it true, what Mrs. Smith said?

Why did Mrs. Smith say this to Jane?

Story type: Figure of Speech

Emma has a cough. All through lunch she coughs and coughs and coughs. Father says, "Poor Emma, you must have a frog in you throat!"

Is it true, what Father says to Emma?

Why does he say that?

Figure 7.3 Examples of the Strange Stories (Happé 1994a).

controls passed first- and second-order theory of mind tasks.

The autistic subjects' intellectual abilities were assessed with WISC–R or WAIS and the MLD controls' with the British Picture Vocabulary Scale. The verbal IQ of the MLD controls ranged from 40 to 89 with a mean of 57. The autistic subjects ranged in verbal IQ from 52 to 101, with means for the three groups as follows: no-theory of mind group 62, first-order theory of mind group 82, second-order theory of mind group 96. While there was a difference in verbal ability between the three autistic groups, all three had higher verbal ability than the MLD controls.

The answers to the test question ("Why did he/she say that?") were scored as either correct or incorrect, and as either involving mental states/psychological factors, or involving physical states. Explanations rated as mental included the following: "Because he doesn't like the dentist", "She's cross", "He's lying", "Said it to fool her", "She's just pretending", "He's making a joke", "He knows they won't believe him", "She doesn't want to upset them". Explanations rated as physical included the following: "So he won't have to go to the dentist", "So she won't get spanked", "Because it looks like a telephone", "In order to sell the kittens", "Because the dog is big", "Because she won the competition".

The most surprising finding from this study was that the autistic subjects as a group gave as many mental state answers as the controls. However, when these mental state answers were examined it became clear that the autistic subjects were using mental terms quite inappropriate to the story contexts. Autistic subjects who failed the theory of mind tests tended to use a single mental state term repeatedly, irrespective of story type. So, for example, one subject gave the answer, "She/he's having a joke" for 15 of the 24 stories (including the Lie, White Lie, Misunderstanding, Persuasion and Forget stories). Another subject repeatedly used the verb "to think", but in such a way that it seemed unlikely that he really understood the meaning of the term: "He thinks a lawnmower cut her hair", "She thinks he keeps pigs in his room", "She thought the book was a rabbit". Many of the autistic subjects showed striking inventiveness in finding some cause in the physical world to explain the speaker's literally-false utterance: one subject explained the white lie about being glad to receive encyclopaedias instead of a rabbit as being "Because the book was all about rabbits". Another subject responded to the figure of speech "a frog in your throat" by saying that the story character had swallowed a frog. An intelligent 24-year-old man explained a story about pretending a banana is a telephone by saying that, "Some cordless telephones are made to look like fruit". These responses give an immediate sense of the autistic person's idiosyncratic view of events, and the relative difficulty for them of attributing mental states, which makes constructing an elaborate and unusual physical explanation the preferred, easier, or perhaps only, option.

Even the intelligent autistic subjects in the second-order theory of mind group made glaring errors, giving context-inappropriate mental state answers. So, for example, one 17-year-old boy of normal intelligence explained a case of sarcasm (where a mother says to her daughter, "Well that's very nice, that's what I call politeness!") with the justification that "The mother said it so as not to shock her daughter". Another subject explained a case of pretence by saying that "The girl said it to trick her friend". Similarly, Double Bluff was explained as "He just wanted to tell the truth". Persuasion, in the story where a woman says she will drown her kittens if the girl does not buy them, was explained as "Just a joke". By contrast, control subjects never gave this sort of context-inappropriate explanation.

The three theory of mind groups of autistic subjects were well discriminated by the Strange Stories. Indeed there was scarcely any overlap in the total number of correct answers given; no-theory of mind autistic subjects gave between six and nine correct explanations (maximum possible was 24), first-order theory of mind autistics gave from 9 to 16, and second-order theory of mind autistic subjects gave from 17 to 21 correct answers. This compares to a range of 17–24 in the MLD controls and 22–24 in the normal adult subjects.

In conclusion, it appeared from this study that there were real underlying differences in the mentalizing ability of the three groups of autistic subjects: performance on standard tests of understanding false belief and deception related closely to performance on the Strange Stories test of communicative understanding. The existence of a subgroup of people with autism who show both better social and better communicative understanding is interesting, and may relate to the increasingly-used diagnosis of Asperger's syndrome (see Ch. 8).

It is perhaps surprising that even those autistic subjects who passed the second-order theory of mind tasks made striking mistakes with some of the Strange Stories. In particular, they made mis-match mental state errors of a type never seen in the normal adults' responses. These errors can be explained as failures to use the story context in order to understand the speaker's utterance. If utterances were taken in isolation, then it would be very hard to choose the correct intention in the Strange Stories task. So, for example, if all you know is that someone said, "It's lovely", you cannot know whether this is an example of sarcasm, compliment, white lie, pretence, double bluff, or joking. Only by integrating all the elements of the story can you decide on the speaker's motivation. This integration process seems to be very hard for people with autism (Frith 1989a), and it may be that additional difficulties of this type limit the usefulness of autistic subjects' mentalizing ability in everyday life (see Ch. 10).

Conclusions

This chapter has explored the underlying cognitive capacities of the "talented minority" of autistic subjects who pass theory of mind tasks. Overall, there seems to be good evidence that at least some subjects with autism are able to represent mental states in certain situations. This ability is manifest in their better everyday social insight and better understanding of nonliteral communication, as well as in consistently correct theory of mind task performance. It remains a puzzle, then, why these individuals are still handicapped in real life. Delay in acquiring mentalizing is one possible explanation. Another possibility is the persistence of some quite separate additional impairment. This idea is taken up again in Chapter 10. A second question is why some people with autism acquire mentalizing ability, while other do not. In the next chapter, we focus on a new diagnostic label being used to mark out a subgroup of relatively able people with autism. The study of "Asperger's syndrome" may, in the future, hold the key to our understanding of the talented minority.

Suggested reading

Happé, F.G.E. 1993. Communicative competence and theory of mind in autism: a test of Relevance theory. *Cognition* **48**, 101–19.

Happé, F.G.E. 1994. An advanced test of theory of mind: understanding of story characters' thoughts and feelings by able autistic, mentally handicapped and normal children and adults. *Journal of Autism and Developmental Disorders* **24**, 129–54.

Schopler, E. & G. B. Mesibov (eds) 1991. *High-functioning individuals with autism.* New York: Plenum Press.

Chapter 8

Asperger's syndrome

Chapter 2 discussed Hans Asperger's observations of a group of children he considered to have "autistic psychopathy". As well as striking similarities to Kanner's first description of his own American cases, Asperger's account contains points which contrast with the Kanner prototype of autism. In particular, his cases appear to have had better language abilities, more motor difficulties and perhaps more original thinking capacities than Kanner's subjects. These differences have led people to wonder whether Asperger was, in fact, describing a rather different group of children – perhaps a special subgroup within the autistic spectrum.

Diagnosis

History

The term "Asperger's syndrome" was first used by Lorna Wing (1981a), who introduced the diagnosis in an attempt to gain recognition for those very able autistic people who do not fit the Kanner stereotype of being silent and aloof. She listed six diagnostic criteria based on Asperger (1944):

1. speech – no delay, but content odd, pedantic, stereotyped;
2. non-verbal communication – little facial expression, monotone voice, inappropriate gesture;
3. social interactions – not reciprocal, lacking empathy;
4. resistance to change – enjoy repetitive activities;
5. motor coordination – gait and posture odd, gross movements clumsy, sometimes stereotypies;
6. skills and interests – good rote memory, circumscribed special interests.
   In addition to these, she reports Asperger's claim that this disorder is

more frequent in males than females, and rarely recognized before the third year of life. Wing modified these criteria, according to her own clinical experience, making three changes:

(i) Language delay – only half of the group Wing would label as having "Asperger's syndrome" developed language at the normal age.

(ii) Early development – before the age of 3 years the child may be odd, e.g. no joint attention.

(iii) Creativity – Wing claims these children are not creative, and for example do not show true pretend play. Rather than being "original", their thought is inappropriate.

This first paper on Asperger's syndrome set the tone for most that followed, in two important ways. First, it suggested that the differences between Kanner-type autism and Asperger's syndrome were to be explained by a difference in severity alone; that is, that Asperger's syndrome subjects are high-ability autistics. Secondly, it began the plethora of papers suggesting criteria for Asperger's syndrome without specifying which features were necessary and sufficient for this diagnosis. Wing's interest in Asperger's syndrome was a pragmatic one; as a useful diagnosis for people not fitting the strict criteria for autism as defined in the *Diagnostic and statistical manual of mental disorders*, 3rd edn (DSM–III: American Psychiatric Association 1980). The criteria in DSM–III were significantly more restrictive than those in the revised edition (DSM–III–R) (American Psychiatric Association 1987), and included onset before age 30 months, a pervasive lack of responsiveness to other people, and gross deficits in language development. These narrow criteria led to the exclusion of subjects who, in Wing's view, should be recognized none the less as autistic. For Wing, then, Asperger's syndrome formed a means of extending the autistic spectrum to previously unrecognized, subtle degrees.

Some authors have denied the usefulness of the label "Asperger's syndrome" (e.g. Volkmar et al. 1985), on the grounds that forming subgroups does not aid recognition that autism has a range of manifestations. However, a number of clinicians have adopted the label, and found it of practical, if not theoretical, use. Most researchers have followed Wing's suggestions fairly closely in their diagnostic criteria for Asperger's syndrome. By the end of the 1980s, something of a consensus seemed to have emerged. Burd & Kerbeshian (1987) offered five features of Asperger's syndrome subjects:

1. speech – pedantic, stereotyped, aprosodic;
2. impaired non-verbal communication;

3. social interaction – peculiar, lacks empathy;
4. circumscribed interests – repetitive activities or savant skills;
5. movements – clumsy or stereotyped.

Tantam (1988a,b), looking at adults with Asperger's syndrome, proposed the same core disabilities in communication, socialization, and non-verbal expression, with conspicuous clumsiness and special interests. Gillberg (1989) required all six of his criteria for a diagnosis of Asperger's syndrome to be made. These criteria are broadly the five used by Tantam and Burd & Kerbeshian, plus a tendency for the individual to impose routine or their special interest on their entire life (recalling Wing's fourth criterion, resistance to change). Using these criteria, Ehlers & Gillberg (1993) found a prevalence of around 4 per 1000, in a total population study of 1519 children (aged 7–16 years) in the mainstream schools of one borough in Sweden.

Some degree of agreement has emerged, then, concerning the core features of Asperger's syndrome. However, inevitably perhaps, some of Asperger's original insights have been lost during this process. Perhaps most importantly, researchers have lost sight of Asperger's conviction that the pattern of impairments he described could occur in children of low intelligence as well as in those of high ability. Many recent proponents of the Asperger's syndrome diagnosis suggest that it should be reserved for higher-functioning people with autism, meaning those without severe learning difficulties (or mental handicap) – see, for example, the proposed 10th edition of the *International classification of diseases* (ICD-10) criteria below.

The diagnosis of Asperger's syndrome has been discussed largely by clinicians, and this may explain the loose approach to the specification of diagnostic criteria. Interest in this diagnosis began primarily in its use as a label for a sort of patient who had hitherto been hard to fit into existing categories, but whom the clinician felt was an easily recognized "type". Much written on the subject of diagnosing Asperger's syndrome, then, can be seen as an attempt by such clinicians to convey an impressionistic feel of a type of patient they believe they could recognize "at first sight". As a result the diagnosis is as yet quite poorly defined, making it hard to assess the results of experimental studies (e.g. Ozonoff et al. 1991b) investigating differences between so-called "Asperger's syndrome" subjects and subjects with autism who do not receive this diagnosis.

Controversies

Szatmari et al. (1989a) have probably made the largest effort towards making the diagnosis of Asperger's syndrome look anything more than narrative. They suggested the criteria shown in Table 8.1.

This system of diagnosis, while it deserves credit for being one of the most systematic currently on offer, is problematic in a number of ways common to most proposed criteria for Asperger's syndrome. For example, the lists of symptoms from which the individual must show a specified number seem to be derived without consideration of underlying handicaps. Describing and requiring behaviour at this surface level is problematic; do Szatmari et al. believe that a subject might show limited facial expression but be able

Table 8.1 Diagnostic criteria for Asperger's syndrome suggested by Szatmari et al. (1989a)

1. **Solitary** – two of:
   no close friends
   avoids others
   no interest in making friends
   a loner

2. **Impaired social interaction** – one of:
   approaches others only to have own needs met
   clumsy social approach
   one-sided responses to peers
   difficulty sensing the feelings of others
   detached from feelings of others

3. **Impaired nonverbal communication** – one of:
   limited facial expression
   unable to read emotion from facial expression
   unable to give message with eyes
   does not look at others
   does not use hands to express self
   gestures large and clumsy
   comes too close to others

4. **Odd speech** – two of:
   abnormal inflection
   talks too much or too little
   lack of cohesion in conversation
   idiosyncratic use of words
   repetitive patterns of speech

5.   **Does not meet DSM–III–R criteria for autistic disorder.**

to "give a message with the eyes"? If so, what sort of an underlying cognitive deficit could give rise to such fractionated symptoms? For this reason, the detail in their diagnostic scheme is actually a disadvantage, since it encourages us to think about surface behaviours rather than underlying deficits that manifest themselves very differently in different individuals, different age groups, and different ability ranges. It might be argued that the lists of alternative behaviours given by Szatmari et al. are an attempt to cover just such a range of manifestations of the same underlying handicap. However, it is far from clear that the same deficit necessarily underlies a person's "difficulty sensing feelings of others" and a person's being "detached from the feelings of others". Similarly, not having close friends may not necessarily be attributable to the same handicap as avoidance of others. The same point can be made about Gillberg's (1991) specification of his six criteria for Asperger's syndrome: it is not clear that "inability to interact with peers" and "lack of desire to interact with peers" should be considered equivalent.

What seems clear is that any diagnostic scheme for Asperger's syndrome cannot actually be free from theory; take the insistence of Szatmari et al. that Asperger's syndrome subjects do not meet criteria for autism in DSM–III–R. This exclusion criterion means that no allowance is made for developmental *change* in the diagnostic picture. Wing (1981a) and others have pointed out that a child may look typically Kanner-type autistic in infancy and yet develop into a more Asperger's syndrome-like adolescent. The fifth criterion specified by Szatmari et al. denies this fact. It therefore makes a theoretical claim about Asperger's syndrome: that to have Asperger's syndrome ever you must have had Asperger's syndrome always. It also takes a theoretical stand on the distinction between Asperger's syndrome and autism.

The future

It needs to be recognized, then, that diagnosis is not theory-free, even when it appears to be so. If this is the case we need to think carefully about diagnosis and theory and how they interact. It is a major problem with most studies of Asperger's syndrome that we cannot be sure to what extent the same sort of population of subjects has been used. We need strict diagnosis for purity of sample in experiments, but our diagnosis presupposes our findings, since to choose our criteria we look to our beliefs about the disorder. Perhaps what is needed is a more preliminary exploration. One approach might be to look for real subgroups in the autistic population (see below). Another approach would be to examine the clinical judgements made: compare individuals diagnosed as having Asperger's syndrome by different clinicians on a number of measures. A third answer is simply to recognize the theoretical biases that drive diagnosis, and then use them more explicitly. A set of criteria for Asperger's syndrome derived openly from theory could be used to define a subject population, which could then be contrasted with some other group on a number of tasks and measures of real-life adaptation.

The criteria for Asperger's syndrome suggested in the draft of ICD–10 (World Health Organization 1990) (see Table 8.2) are unlikely to clarify the diagnosis. As can be seen, Asperger's syndrome seems to be defined as autism without the language and cognitive impairments. Note that this carries the theoretical implication that the language and cognitive impairments in autism are not fundamental to the disorder, and do not arise from the same underlying deficit as the social difficulties. The implication is that the language and cognitive impairments are additional handicaps, which can be present with or without autism, and leave the picture of "core" (i.e. social?) handicaps unchanged in their absence. Asperger's syndrome in this document is said to include "at least some cases" which "represent mild varieties of autism". The unspoken message here is that mild autism equals mild retardation and mild language difficulties. However, it might be argued that mild autism means a mild degree of social handicap. If so, then normal IQ should not be a criterion (as it is: "a lack of any clinically significant general delay in . . . cognitive development"), until it has been shown that it is impossible to have mild autism and low IQ. This may or may not be the case; it is an empirical question. Against the claim is Szatmari & Jones's (1991) conclusion, from a review of work on IQ and genetics, that "the IQ of an autistic child does not index severity of autism".

In ICD–10, autism is diagnosed if the subject meets a certain number of criteria out of a list of possible behaviours. This leads to problems of differential diagnosis when we consider Asperger's syndrome. Why is Asperger's syndrome needed when there is a category of "atypical autism", which allows a child to fail to fit full criteria for autism (so the child might show symptoms late, might have some social skills, or relatively normal language ability)? In any case, most Asperger's syndrome people would probably fit the ICD–10 Autism diagnosis itself. For example, under the section on communication in the ICD–10 criteria for Autism, a person needs only two out of the five impairments listed to be diagnosed autistic. Of these five, one would expect most Asperger's syndrome people to show at least the following three items: relative failure to initiate/sustain conversation, abnormality of prosody, lack of varied spontaneous make-believe play. Similarly, the person with Asperger's syndrome could fit the required three out of five symptoms of social impairment, and so on. The only strong distinctions in the diagnosis of Asperger's syndrome seem to be age of onset and lack of language delay. Both of these are dubious, because they depend in general on indirect report, and because they do not allow for developmental dynamics. The criteria for language development, in particular, are both too specific and too vague in an area about which we know so little: "Diagnosis requires that single words should have developed by two years of age or earlier and that communicative phrases be used by three years of age or earlier". This diagnostic requirement is not based on any recognized theory of normal language acquisition, and is not precise – it is not clear what is to be considered a word, how many must be acquired, or what counts as a communicative phrase. The implication of this criterion is, once again, that the failure of most autistic children to develop language normally is quite separate from their failure in social development. Chapters 5 and 7 discuss why this assumption is very likely to be wrong: communicative and social development are likely to rely on at least one common mechanism – the ability to attribute mental states. In addition, the language criteria in ICD–10 appear to be impractical, since, as Ehlers & Gillberg (1993) say, "it is usually impossible to determine with accuracy in a school age child whether single words had been present at age 2 years and communicative phrases at age 3 years". Indeed, in these authors' epidemiological study several children could not be given a firm ICD–10 diagnosis of Asperger's syndrome, simply due to the lack of sufficiently detailed developmental information.

ICD–10, as it stands, excludes from the diagnosis of Asperger's syndrome cases where an autistic childhood gives way to Asperger's syndrome in adulthood. There is not, as yet, any proof to back such a decision; one would need to show that such adults are very different from those who have had an Asperger's syndrome childhood. However, if diagnosis "jumps the gun" in this way, such important questions will never be answered, because the populations used for research will be selected according to prejudicial criteria. For this reason, Ghaziuddin et al. (1992a) may be over-optimistic in their conclusion (from a brief comparison of the diagnostic criteria suggested by different authors) that "at the risk of being somewhat rigid and narrow, the ICD–10 criteria attempt to create a homogenous category

Table 8.2   Criteria for Asperger's syndrome in ICD-10 (draft, World Health Organization 1990).

A. A lack of any clinically significant general delay in language or cognitive development. Diagnosis requires that single words should have developed by two years of age or earlier and that communicative phrases be used by three years of age or earlier. Self-help skills, adaptive behaviour and curiosity about the environment during the first three years should be at a level consistent with normal intellectual development. However, motor milestones may be somewhat delayed and motor clumsiness is usual (although not a necessary diagnostic feature). Isolated special skills, often related to abnormal preoccupations, are common, but are not required for diagnosis.

B. Qualitative impairments in reciprocal social interaction (criteria as for autism). Diagnosis requires demonstrable abnormalities in at least three out of the following five areas:

1. failure adequately to use eye-to-eye gaze, facial expression, body posture and gesture to regulate social interaction;

2. failure to develop (in a manner appropriate to mental age, and despite ample opportunities) peer relationships that involve a mutual sharing of interests, activities and emotions;

3. rarely seeking and using other people for comfort and affection at times of stress or distress and/or offering comfort and affection to others when they are showing distress or unhappiness;

4. lack of shared enjoyment in terms of vicarious pleasure in other people's happiness and/or a spontaneous seeking to share their own enjoyment through joint involvement with others;

5. a lack of socio-emotional reciprocity as shown by an impaired or deviant response to other people's emotions; and/or lack of modulation of behaviour according to social context, and/or a weak integration of social, emotional and communicative behaviours.

C. Restricted, repetitive, and stereotyped patterns of behaviour, interests and activities (criteria as for autism; however it would be less usual for these to include either motor mannerisms or preoccupations with part-objects or non-functional elements of play materials). Diagnosis requires demonstrable abnormalities in at least two out of the following six areas:

1. an encompassing preoccupation with stereotyped and restricted patterns of interest;

2. specific attachments to unusual objects;

3. apparently compulsive adherence to specific, non-functional, routines or rituals;

4. stereotyped and repetitive motor mannerisms that involve either hand/finger flapping or twisting, or complex whole body movements;

5. preoccupations with part-objects or non-functional elements of play materials (such as their odour, the feel of their surface, or the noise/vibration that they generate);

6. distress over changes in small, non-functional, details of the environment.

D. The disorder is not attributable to the other varieties of pervasive developmental disorder; schizotypal disorder; simple schizophrenia; reactive and disinhibited attachment disorder of childhood; obsessional personality disorder; obsessive-compulsive disorder.

which may further our understanding of subtypes of pervasive developmental disorders".

Asperger's syndrome and autism: how different is different enough?

There seems to be good reason to connect Asperger's syndrome and autism, despite the suggestion by Wolff (see Ch. 9) that Asperger's own subjects were more akin to children with schizoid disorders than to those with autism. It appears that some individuals with classic "Kanner-type" autism in childhood develop into teenagers and adults with Asperger's syndrome (Wing 1981a). In addition, a growing number of family studies have found the co-occurrence of Asperger's syndrome and autism in the same family to be higher than expected by chance. Bowman (1988) reports a family in which the four sons and the father all show differing degrees of autistic handicap – from the mildest case, which looks like Asperger's syndrome, to the most severe, a typical "Kanner case" where autism is compounded by mental retardation. Similarly, Burgoine & Wing (1983) report a set of triplets who span the range from Asperger's syndrome to classic Kanner-type autism. Eisenberg (1957) gives a description of some of the fathers of autistic children, which is highly reminiscent of accounts of Asperger's syndrome adults – and recalls Asperger's conviction that the parents of his subjects showed similar traits to their Asperger's syndrome children. DeLong & Dwyer (1988) examined 929 first- and second-degree relatives of 51 children with autism, and found a high incidence of Asperger's syndrome in the families of autistic children with near-normal intelligence (IQ above 70) but not in the families of more handicapped children. Most recently, Gillberg (1991) has described the families of six Asperger's syndrome individuals between the ages of 6 and 33 years. He found that two of the families had a first-degree relative afflicted with autism. In addition, Asperger's syndrome or

Asperger-like traits could be identified in at least one first- or second-degree relative of each of the children. Across the six families he found that three of the mothers, four of the fathers, one brother and one paternal grandfather were affected.

Establishing that there is a connection between autism and Asperger's syndrome raises questions of differential diagnosis. First, is Asperger's syndrome a distinct (if related) disorder from autism? If "yes", what is the distinction, and does it warrant recognition – does it have implications for management, education and prognosis? If "no", is Asperger's syndrome simply a label for all autistic people with relatively high IQ, or should it apply to a specific subset of more able individuals with autism?

Asperger, by 1979, felt sure that the children he described were in a separate category from Kanner's children with "early infantile autism", although he recognized that the two groups had much in common. He put forward as distinguishing characteristics the fact that his subjects had good logical and "abstract" thought, good surface language (vocabulary, phonology, syntax, and so on), and a better prognosis than Kanner's subjects. These three features might be explained by higher IQ alone, but Asperger insisted that the syndrome he described could occur at *all* IQ levels, from the "genius" to the "automata-like mentally retarded" (Asperger 1944, translated in Frith 1991b). For example, Hellmuth (described by Asperger in his original 1944 paper) showed the characteristic features of "autistic psychopathy", despite brain damage and mental handicap.

Van Krevelen (1971) follows Asperger in making a strong bid for the independence of Asperger's syndrome. According to him, "autistic psychopathy" and Kanner's autism are "two entirely different nosological syndromes" – though he does admit there are connections, such as the familial co-occurrence. The crucial difference, in Van Krevelen's view, is the child's attitude to others; autistic children act as if others did not exist, while children with Asperger's syndrome evade other people, of whom they are aware. It is interesting to note that Van Krevelen's description stresses much more than does Asperger's the child's visuospatial problems (for example in judging distances), maths inability and clumsiness – giving a picture strikingly reminiscent of the "right-hemisphere learning disabilities" discussed in the next chapter. The full set of differences proposed by Van Krevelen can be seen in Table 8.3. He concludes that autism results when there is the genetic predisposition for Asperger's syndrome plus the occurrence of brain damage.

Kanner is not known to have expressed an opinion on Asperger's syn-

Table 8.3   Van Krevelen's distinguishing features of Asperger's syndrome.

Early Infantile Autism	Autistic Psychopathy
1. Manifestation age: first month of life	Manifestation age: third year or later.
2. Child walks earlier than he speaks; speech is retarded or absent.	Child walks late, speaks earlier.
3. Language does not attain the function of communication.	Language aims at communication but remains "one-way traffic".
4. Eye contact: other people do not exist.	Eye contact: other people are evaded.
5. The child lives in a world of his own.	The child lives in our world in his own way.
6. Social prognosis is poor.	Social prognosis is rather good.
7. A psychotic process.	A personality trait.

drome, or its relation to autism as he defined it. However, Burd & Kerbeshian (1987) quote Kanner's commentary on Robinson & Vitale's (1954) report of children with circumscribed interest patterns, in which he says that these children do not fit his definition of autism. Burd & Kerbeshian claim that these children would fit the description of Asperger's syndrome.

More recently, Szatmari et al. (1986) have presented a case study to support the claim that "not all children with Asperger's syndrome are autistic, at least as judged by early history and prognosis". However, the question again arises of how narrow a definition of autism is appropriate. Their subject, Mary, had no language delay, but otherwise sounds fairly typically autistic. The authors claim that Mary's outcome – she developed auditory hallucinations during adolescence – makes it unlikely that she was autistic. This is something of a presumption: there have been reports in the literature of subjects who perfectly fulfil the criteria for autism in childhood, but who go on to develop schizophrenia later in life (Petty et al. 1984, Watkin et al. 1988).

Experimental studies have failed to reveal any very striking differences between groups of autistic and groups of "Asperger's syndrome" children. This is due in part, no doubt, to the problem of diagnosis. It would not be an exaggeration to say that no study to date has satisfactorily defined and distinguished populations of Asperger's syndrome and of "non-Asperger's syndrome" autistic children. This, in its turn, is not surprising. There is not only the problem of a lack of agreed diagnostic criteria, there is also the more insidious problem of defining groups on the basis of fractionated surface behaviours alone, without thought to underlying deficits and their necessary and sufficient manifestations at the symptom level.

Szatmari et al. (1990) compared "high-functioning" autistic subjects, Asperger's syndrome subjects and an outpatient control group on a number of tasks. The diagnostic criteria for Asperger's syndrome were isolated behaviour, odd speech/non-verbal communication/preoccupations, impaired social relations, and onset before age 6 years. It is not clear in what way the high-functioning autistic group did *not* conform to this description. Unfortunately, IQ matching of the experimental groups in this study led to a significant difference in age, the high-functioning autistic children being significantly older than the Asperger's syndrome group. In addition, the controls were significantly brighter than the experimental groups. Few major differences emerged between the Asperger's syndrome and high-functioning autism groups, although both were very different from the controls. The majority of the differences that reached significance were found in the answers mothers gave about their child's history – which is problematic since it seems plausible that a better outcome may lead parents to remember the former years in a more positive light. Szatmari et al. found that more mothers of high-functioning autistic than of Asperger's syndrome children reported their child to lack social responsiveness to them, to have a complete lack of interest in social relations, to show echolalia, repetitive speech and stereotypies, and to show no imaginative play. More Asperger's syndrome than high-functioning autistic children showed affection as a baby, shared their special interest with their parents, and enjoyed the company of adults other than their parents – according to the mothers' report. Interestingly, no major difference emerged on pegboard tests for motor skills, arguing against claims that Asperger's syndrome is distinguished from autism by clumsiness. A lack of any striking difference was also found in a study of early history and outcome with these subject groups (Szatmari et al. 1989). Echolalia, pronoun reversal, global social impairment and restricted activity were more common in high-functioning autistic children. Perhaps the only finding of note, and not easily explained by a failure to match subject groups on verbal IQ, was that the Asperger's syndrome group were more likely to develop a secondary psychiatric disorder than were the high-functioning autistic subjects. Szatmari et al. conclude that "there were no substantive, qualitative differences between the Asperger's syndrome and autistic groups, indicating that Asperger's syndrome should be considered a mild form of high-functioning autism".

Ozonoff et al. (1991), by contrast, in a study of differences between an Asperger's syndrome group and a high-functioning autistic group, concluded that an empirical distinction could be made. Their subjects were matched on age, performance IQ and full-scale IQ, but differed significantly on verbal IQ (Asperger's syndrome subjects exceeding high-functioning autistic subjects). Ozonoff and her colleagues found that both groups were impaired relative to controls on executive function tasks and emotion perception, but that only the high-functioning autistic group showed significant impairments on theory of mind tasks and memory tasks. The authors conclude from this that high-functioning autism and Asperger's syndrome are empirically distinguishable on measures independent of diagnostic criteria, and that theory of mind impairment cannot be the primary handicap in autism (since it is not pervasive throughout the continuum to Asperger's syndrome). Instead, they claim that there are unifying deficits in autistic and Asperger's syndrome subjects which point to frontal lobe damage (see Ch. 6). However, these otherwise unusually clear findings are clouded by questions of diagnosis. The diagnosis of Asperger's syndrome was made on the basis of current symptoms only, and yet Ozonoff et al. claim to have used ICD–10 criteria for diagnosis. It is hard to see how ICD–10 could be applied with any rigour without information on history and especially language development in these subjects, given ICD–10's strict criteria of no language delays. In fact, the authors report that half of their Asperger's syndrome subjects had typical autistic language symptoms and developmental delays. Evidently, if we cannot be sure of the diagnosis in this study, the findings – although interesting in themselves and useful perhaps in the search for subtypes – cannot tell us conclusively whether Asperger's syndrome is a distinct subtype of autism.

Is Asperger's syndrome just high-functioning autism?

Accepting the conclusion of Szatmari et al. that Asperger's syndrome is just a mild form of autism does not solve the puzzle of Asperger's syndrome. What does it really mean to say that Asperger's syndrome is a "mild form of high-functioning autism"? Is Asperger's syndrome *a* mild form of high-functioning autism, or *the* mild form of high-functioning autism? What must be decided, in other words, is whether there are *other* "mild forms of high-functioning autism" which *are not* Asperger's syndrome.

Most researchers have come to much the same conclusion as Szatmari and his colleagues, and are content to explain the differences between Asperger's syndrome and autism on the basis of severity. This explanation implicitly suggests that there could not be other types of able autistic person. If Asperger's syndrome people are different from other, more Kanner-type autistics only because of a "milder" handicap, then *any* autistic person with a similarly mild handicap will (by definition) have Asperger's syndrome. This is implicit in Wing's (1981a) conclusion that there is no distinction between Asperger's syndrome and higher-level autism, being just part of the autistic continuum. At the same time she argues that Asperger's syndrome is useful practically, as a label for *less typical* autistic people, who do not fit the pattern of the child who is "agile, but aloof and indifferent to others, with little or no speech and no eye contact". One might take the stance that this very "atypicality" – in more than just IQ – suggests there might be subgroups of "mild autism", but Wing argues that all the differences can be explained by severity and ability level.

Other researchers have claimed that Asperger's syndrome is a distinguishable group even defined as the group at the upper end of the ability (or the lower end of the severity) spectrum. Gillberg (1989) compared 23 Swedish children with Asperger's syndrome against 23 autistic children, matched for IQ and age (range 5–18 years). As previously, it is not clear in what respects the autistic children did not fit Gillberg's criteria for Asperger's syndrome. Gillberg finds the following differences: the frequency of Asperger's syndrome-like problems in the parents was higher for the Asperger's syndrome children (57 versus 13 per cent); motor clumsiness was more common in the Asperger's syndrome children (83 versus 22 per cent), despite the fact that Gillberg did not include this as a diagnostic criterion in this study; circumscribed interests were found in 99 per cent of the Asperger's syndrome cases and only 30 per cent of the autistics – probably largely due to his diagnostic criteria for Asperger's syndrome, which included "special interests". No differences emerged on the neurobiological tests. Gillberg and his colleagues (Gillberg et al. 1987, Gillberg 1989) concluded that Asperger's syndrome subjects are "different in the sense that they are not so pervasively impaired as Kanner-autism 'prototype' children". It is not clear how the greater clumsiness of the Asperger's syndrome subjects in Gillberg's study fits this idea of lesser impairment. However, a recent review of the literature concluded that clumsiness as a symptom of Asperger's syndrome has not been adequately studied (Ghaziuddin et al. 1992b), and to date there is little experimental evidence of significant, objectively assessed motor impairments specific to these subjects.

Heterogeneity among high-functioning individuals with autism?

Most researchers, then, seem quite happy to say that Asperger's syndrome is a label for high-functioning autistic individuals. But what is meant by terms such as "high functioning" and "able autistic"? Newson et al. (1984a,b) studied a large group of "able autistics" contacted through a national advertising campaign, and report a very varied picture. Insistence on sameness, for example, was seen to widely varying degrees among autistic people of apparently equal "ability". This great variation, even among those autistics who have a relatively mild handicap, suggests that by no means all of the Newson group would be described as having Asperger's syndrome. For example, only four out of the total of 93 parents could say that they had *not* been concerned about the development of language, and only 27 of the 93 autistic subjects had reached the two-word stage by age 3 years. By the proposed ICD–10 criteria for autism, at least, few of the Newson sample would have received a diagnosis of Asperger's syndrome.

A study by Rumsey & Hamburger (1988) also suggests that there is a group of "high-functioning" autistic individuals who do not fit the description of Asperger's syndrome. They compared 10 "able autistic" men of normal IQ with 10 "normal" controls. Tests revealed no differences in motor skills between the groups. The authors stress the "similarity between the Wechsler profile for [their] sample and that of lower functioning samples (Lockyer and Rutter 1970)". This result strongly suggests that high ability, in terms of IQ at least, is *not* enough to transform a typical autistic picture into an Asperger's syndrome picture. Equally, Tantam (1988a,b) found adults whom he diagnosed as having Asperger's syndrome, who had low intellectual ability. Gillberg et al. (1986) report a rate of Asperger's syndrome within a "mentally retarded" population that approximates the prevalence found among children at "normal" schools in Ehlers & Gillberg's (1993) epidemiological study.

It seems, then, that a "mild form of high-functioning autism" is not necessarily Asperger's syndrome – one may have a relatively mild handicap and be autistic *without* conforming to the Asperger's syndrome subtype. This suggests that a very fruitful line of research may be the exploration of significantly distinct subgroups within the autistic spectrum. One such study, by Volkmar et al. (1989), used Wing's subtypes of "aloof", "passive" and "active but odd" social behaviour to categorize a group of autistic spectrum children. Although these styles of social impairment can be shown concurrently by the same child in different situations, the authors (like Wing & Gould 1979) were able to assign subjects to one of the three groups on the basis of predominant style of social behaviour. The results are interesting and should encourage specific investigation of such subtypes, with the diagnosis of Asperger's syndrome in mind. The authors found significant differences between the children in the three social impairment subgroups. For example, social type was strongly related to IQ, with "active" children most and "aloof" children least intelligent. Special abilities were significantly more common (80 per cent prevalence) in the "active" group. Siegel et al. (1986) also looked for subtypes among autistic and "autistic-like" children, on the basis of current functioning. They derived four groups which they claim are an advance on current diagnostic categories, since they identify co-occurring behaviours and assign children to more homogenous subtypes. Although Siegel et al.'s subjects were grouped on the basis of current functioning, the groups derived also differed in history of pre- and perinatal problems, and early development. Asperger's syndrome approximates most closely to subtype 3, characterized by better language, and some schizoid features (e.g. bizarre ideas).

Asperger's syndrome and theory of mind

Throughout this chapter I have argued that theory must inform the search for Asperger's syndrome. I believe that the theory of mind explanation of autism is a particularly good theoretical instrument for this job, since it allows us to move from a continuum of social, communicative and imaginative handicaps in behaviour to a discrete ability that subjects may either lack or possess. It may therefore be possible to go from quantitative differences in surface behaviours to qualitative differences in cognitive deficits. Importantly, such distinctions are likely to have significant implications for prognosis, education and management.

Using theory of mind to guide the diagnosis of Asperger's syndrome might lead to the following suggestion, which could be tested experimentally. "Asperger's syndrome" could be used to refer to those people (discussed in Ch. 7) who gain metarepresentation and theory of mind, perhaps after a significant and damaging delay. Like other autistic people, they lack theory of mind in their early years, and hence fail to develop normal social interaction, and normal perception and expression of internal states. Eventually, these people develop a theory of mind not unlike a normal child's – due to internal or external factors. This ability, however, will have missed its "critical period" and be too late to inform or "tune up" the various perceptual and cognitive systems that normally develop alongside theory of mind in the young child. The Asperger's syndrome person's theory of mind, then, will not be useful in the normal way; it will allow them to pass tests where vital elements are made unnaturally salient, but it will not allow them to solve the more subtle theory of mind problems encountered in everyday social situations. Thus, they will fail to apply their hard-won theory of mind skills in real life. Asperger's syndrome people, then, will still show characteristic (if milder) autistic social impairments in everyday life, despite "real" success on theory of mind tests. They will, however, have a better prognosis, and the type of skills they need to be taught would be meaningfully different from those of other people with autism (who lack theory of mind). Communication will be better in these Asperger's syndrome subjects – although a similar discrepancy between test performance and real-life competence might be expected. The incidence of special interests might be due in part to better ability to tell people about their interests, and a greater desire to fit in (leading, for example, to an interest in carrots rather than in spinning and twiddling objects).

The higher incidence of psychiatric disorders in this group (Tantam 1991, Szatmari et al. 1989b) is well explained by this hypothesis. Depression will be more common since these people have greater insight into their own difficulties and their own feelings and thoughts. Positive symptoms of psychosis, such as hallucinations and delusions would be found *only* in Asperger's syndrome cases by this account, if one takes Frith & Frith's (1991) view of these symptoms as resulting from an "over-active" theory of mind. Asperger's syndrome people, who gain theory of mind late and therefore abnormally, may be at high risk for having their theory of mind "go wrong". On this hypothesis it would be impossible for a Kanner-type autistic person (who has no theory of mind) to show these psychotic or positive symptoms. In this sense (according to Frith & Frith's theory) Asperger's syndrome would be something of a midpoint between autism and (positive or florid) schizophrenia; while the former is due to a lack of theory of mind, and the latter due to over-active theory of mind, some people with Asperger's syndrome may show both the scars of early lack and the florid symptoms of late acquired theory of mind working abnormally hard.

There is some preliminary evidence to support the suggestion that the term "Asperger's syndrome" could meaningfully be restricted to those subjects with autism who have achieved some ability to think about thoughts. Ozonoff et al. (1991) found that their group labelled (perhaps arguably) as having Asperger's syndrome did not show impairments relative to controls on simple tests of (first- and second-order) theory of mind. This distinguished them from the "high-functioning autistic" subjects tested by Ozonoff et al. Similarly, Bowler (1992) found that a group of adults diagnosed by clinicians as having Asperger's syndrome (again on unspecified diagnostic criteria) were no worse than schizophrenics or normal subjects on two second-order theory of mind tasks.

Conclusions

At present "Asperger's syndrome" is probably a term more useful for the practical needs of the clinician, than for the experimental needs of the researcher. Experimental work to date would seem to indicate that the Asperger's syndrome label is used to mark a subgroup of autism which is at the more able end of the spectrum in terms of social and communication handicaps.

The theory of mind explanation has been suggested here as a tool for distinguishing meaningful subgroups, but the more important point is that a hypothesis of some sort should guide the exploration of Asperger's syndrome. Testing groups of subjects labelled as having "Asperger's syndrome" by clinicians cannot be a helpful way to proceed until we have at least a consensus on the necessary and sufficient criteria for this diagnosis. And we are unlikely to reach a satisfactory diagnostic scheme for Asperger's syndrome until we look beyond surface behaviours to the underlying cognitive handicaps. ICD–10, for example, is in danger of excluding, without good theoretical or empirical grounds, those children who change from a Kanner- to an Asperger-type picture in adolescence.

Is there any escape from this "chicken-and-egg" situation between diagnosis and research? Perhaps researchers should look for meaningful subgroups in the population of autistic people and those individuals with related disorders. Theory should guide the search for subgroups, and clinical experience should tell us which subgroups deserve a label. Clinicians may feel the need to continue using Asperger's syndrome to label a (for them) "recognizable" subtype of autism – but researchers will probably make little progress using definitions and diagnostic criteria as confused and confusing as currently appear in the literature on Asperger's syndrome.

Suggested reading

Frith, U. (ed.) 1991. *Autism and Asperger syndrome*. Cambridge: Cambridge University Press.

Ghaziuddin, M., L. Y. Tsai & N. Ghaziuddin 1992. Brief report: a comparison of the diagnostic criteria for Asperger syndrome. *Journal of Autism and Developmental Disorders* **22**, 643–9.

Chapter 9
Autism and not-autism

In this chapter, the nature of autism is explored once again through what it is *not*. This leads on to more practical issues: can a child be partly autistic? What is the relationship of autism to other diagnoses? Do children ever grow out of autism, and can autism be cured?

Mild autism and autistic-like behaviour

Is it meaningful to describe a child as autistic-like, or as having "autistic features" but not being autistic? The triad of handicaps which defines autism is not simply a chance co-occurrence of behaviours, as Wing & Gould (1979) showed. Instead the three impairments co-occur and cohere, to form a true syndrome. This suggests that one core cognitive impairment causes all three handicaps. What does it mean, then, to say that a child is "a bit autistic"?

People who call a child "autistic-like" are probably expressing a number of concerns:

(a) The child they describe may be atypical, and not conform to a Kanner stereotype of autism: he may have a lot of speech (though poor communication), or may be socially interested (but odd in his interaction). In this case, the term "autistic-like" is used to avoid the stereotype of the silent and aloof autistic child. This is probably not a useful way of talking about autism, because by using the term "autistic-like" for such children we are maintaining an incorrect stereotype of the way in which autism can be manifest. The term is also imprecise and the child so labelled may not receive the educational rights which a diagnosis of autism should confer.

(b) The child they describe may be more able than most autistic children. In this case there may be reason for talking about "mild autism", but "autistic-like" implies a fundamental handicap other than autism that merely resembles autism – and this is misleading.

(c) The term may be used to refer to some of the child's behaviour only; the child is seen, for example, as having "autistic-like" communication problems. This use of the term ignores the concept of autism as a true syndrome, caused by a fundamental cognitive impairment which is manifest in the *triad* of impairments. A child who shows communication problems but not imagination and socialization handicaps is not autistic, since autism is defined by the co-occurrence of the triad. A child with just a communication problem is just that – a child with a communication problem. It makes no more sense to call this child autistic-like (if the child has normal social and pretend-play skills), than it would to call a person with spots "measles-like". Any one of the triad of impairments alone does not define autism, and so an isolated social handicap, a pure communication handicap, or a problem with imagination alone, should be called such. This is altogether less confusing, and more informative – any one element of the triad on its own is likely to be due to a quite different impairment from that underlying autism.

Differential diagnosis

In Chapter 3, it was argued that autism is a true syndrome, not just a collection of handicaps which co-occur by chance. This implies that autism is a distinct disorder – distinct from normality and distinct from other disorders. How easy is it, in practice, to tell autism and other disorders apart?

Autism appears in a great range of manifestations – a spectrum of disorders. Autism is perhaps easiest to recognize in individuals at the midpoint of this spectrum. Cases at either extreme present a problem for diagnosis: at the low-ability end of the spectrum it may be hard to diagnose autism because the individual's level of functioning is so poor that social, communicative and imaginative functioning may be very low but still in line with the general developmental level (e.g. below 20 months). At the upper end of the spectrum, autistic people may have devised coping strategies which disguise their real problems – as with the autistic adolescent who greets visitors to the school so nicely that they question the diagnosis of autism, but who repeats exactly the same greeting in a stereotyped way 20 times a day to people he already knows!

In addition to the social immaturity which is a part of severe learning difficulties, and the social awkwardness of normal shyness, there exist other suggested diagnoses which appear to resemble autism. Asperger's syndrome has already been discussed, in Chapter 8. Here we turn to other suggested diagnostic categories which may form the borderlands of autism. The validity of these possible syndromes, and their relationship to autism, is as yet unclear, but it may be helpful to look briefly at some of these disorders.

Semantic–pragmatic disorder

Semantic–pragmatic disorder, first discussed by Rapin & Allen (1983), became a popular diagnosis among speech therapists in the mid-1980s. In 1984 and 1985, letters and reports appeared in the *College of Speech Therapists Bulletin*, describing groups of children with severe language problems of a type hard to classify in terms of existing diagnoses. Children were described who showed comprehension problems, echolalia, verbal conceptual deficits, and an inability to use gestures. In addition, some of the children showed severe early behaviour problems and a poverty of symbolic play. Despite obvious similarities, many speech therapists insisted that at least some of these children were not autistic. However, in many cases, this judgement was based on the claim that the children were not withdrawn, and were affectionate. This suggests that too narrow a conception of autism, or too strong an adherence to a Kanner-type stereotype, may have led these authors to discard a diagnosis of autism prematurely. Children with "semantic–pragmatic disorder" are sometimes described as egocentric, with poor social skills making them incapable of getting on with their peers, instead showing affection only to adults. Such descriptions are reminiscent of Asperger's original cases. Nothing in the exploration of these children by Bishop & Adams (1989) (and Adams & Bishop 1989) contradicts the idea that their problems resemble autism or Asperger's syndrome. Indeed, Brook & Bowler (1992), after reviewing empirical studies of children with semantic and pragmatic impairments, concluded that these children could be considered to lie within the autistic continuum.

In an article discussing the boundaries between autism, Asperger's syndrome and semantic–pragmatic disorder, Bishop (1989) suggests that a continuum approach should be taken in this area. She suggests not just a single continuum of severity, but two dimensions, in order to capture the differences in *pattern* of symptoms between the disorders (see Fig. 9.1). This

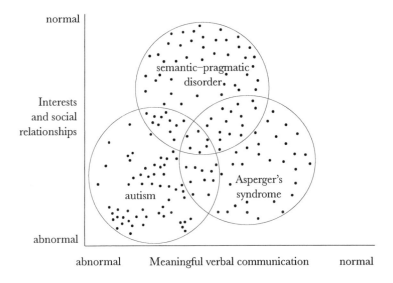

Figure 9.1 Bishop's (1989) dimensional approach to differential diagnosis (by kind permission of the author and publisher).

is an advance on other approaches, and Bishop shows great sensitivity to the issue of the diverse manifestations of social handicap. Autism, Asperger's syndrome and semantic–pragmatic disorder can, for her, be represented as different but overlapping areas on a graph where the *x*-axis is "meaningful verbal communication", and the *y*-axis represents "interests and social relations" (both ranging from "abnormal" to "normal"). However, this presupposes that there is no *necessary* relation between social and communicative competence – since such a graph would be pointless if all subjects with mild social deficits necessarily had mild communicative deficits and so on. This assumption may be incorrect – there is good reason to believe (see Chs 5 & 7) that social and communicative abilities may rely on many of the same cognitive mechanisms. Further research is necessary, however, to assess whether communication problems (in the area of pragmatics, rather than language itself) can be found in children without any degree of autistic social and imagination impairment. Only if this can be shown to be the case will the term "semantic–pragmatic disorder" have a useful rôle to play.

Right hemisphere learning disabilities

The literature on developmental right hemisphere problems has recently been reviewed by Semrud-Clikeman & Hynd (1990), who document a vast array of supposedly distinct syndromes that involve social, motor and visuospatial deficits. The connection of these deficits with the right hemisphere is made largely by analogy to cases of adults who have suffered brain injuries. Extrapolating from the behaviour of an adult who has incurred damage to a fully developed cognitive system to that of a child who's capacities have developed in the absence of a particular cognitive component is a road replete with pitfalls. However, the pattern of symptoms shown by so-called right hemisphere learning disabled children is still of interest in its own right, whatever the site of damage.

Weintraub & Mesulam (1983) discuss 14 children with social and visuospatial problems, and neurological "soft signs" of right hemisphere damage. The four case histories given are certainly reminiscent of autism. Of the 14 children, all showed gaze avoidance, 11 used little or no gesture, 12 had monotone voices, and 13 were described as "shy". The authors conclude: "There is a syndrome of early right hemisphere dysfunction that may be genetically determined and that is associated with introversion, poor social perception, chronic emotional difficulties, inability to display affect, and impairment in visuospatial representation".

Not surprisingly, it was not long before researchers pointed out the similarity between this picture and the clumsiness, odd speech and poor social interaction of autistic children, and specifically of those with Asperger's syndrome (Denckla 1983, DeLeon et al. 1986). Certainly Voeller's (1986) description of one little boy with right hemisphere deficits, travelling in a car with his class mates, sounds very like one of Asperger's cases: "they were all talking about ball games, and he was talking about the way train signals worked".

A similar sort of child seems to have been recognized in an earlier paper by Johnson & Myklebust (1971) on "non-verbal learning disability". They describe such children as unable to comprehend the significant aspects of their environment, lacking the ability to pretend or anticipate, and showing problems with gesture and facial expression. Why did these authors, who recognized that these children had a "social perception" disability, not simply diagnose them as autistic? The answer probably lies in part in the narrow conception of autism still held by many clinicians. The argument has been made that we should be making diagnostic categories progressively narrower, to clarify research findings and make equivalent the results from different studies. However, it seems true to say that different manifestations of the same underlying handicap should be grouped together. That is, we would not change a person's diagnosis just because he was older, or no longer quite so impaired. The question is, then, what is a matter of degree, and what is really a qualitatively different disorder?

Childhood schizophrenia and schizoid personality disorder

The term "autistic" was first used by Bleuler (1908) to describe the social withdrawal seen in people suffering from schizophrenia. Perhaps it is not surprising, then, that for some time autism was believed to have strong links with schizophrenia, and indeed up to the late 1960s was used interchangeably with a diagnosis of "childhood schizophrenia" (for a review of this confusion, see Rutter 1978). Since then, autism has been shown not to be connected with schizophrenia in any straightforward way (Kay & Kolvin 1987). Autistic people are not especially likely to become schizophrenic, nor is schizophrenia particularly prevalent among the relations of people with autism.

However, links between research into schizophrenia and into autism still exist. Frith & Frith (1991) have pointed out the similarities between the negative symptoms of schizophrenia (e.g. emotional blunting), and the handicaps seen in autism. They suggest that a similar cognitive deficit – specifically in theory of mind (see Ch. 5) – might underlie both disorders. The great differences in appearance of the two disorders would be expected: breakdown of a mature cognitive system will not have the same effects as the lack of a cognitive component from the start of development. Chris Frith (1992) also suggests that the positive symptoms of schizophrenia (e.g. hallucinations and delusions) might follow from the abnormal working of the mentalizing component, leading the individual to over-attribute intentions, for example, as in ideas of reference (e.g. believing that the television presenter's words are intended specially for you).

A second link between schizophrenia and autism has come about through Asperger's syndrome. Sula Wolff and her colleagues (e.g. Wolff & Barlow 1979, Wolff & Chick 1980) have studied a group of children with what they call "schizoid personality disorder", who are oversensitive, emotionally detached, solitary, rigid/obsessive, lacking in empathy, and prone to bizarre thoughts. They claim that these are the sort of children Asperger was describing in his 1944 paper. Wolff argues, therefore, that Asperger's syndrome does not belong within the autistic spectrum, but rather is part of the group of schizotypal or schizoid disorders.

Wolff's initial description of schizoid personality disorder, in 1964, did not refer to Asperger's paper (Wolff & Chess 1964). However, she was careful to distinguish her group from autistic children on the basis of three features. She claimed that the schizoid children – unlike those with autism – did *not* show any of the following: a lack of emotional responsiveness and gaze avoidance, ritualistic behaviour, and late/poor language acquisition with echolalia. It is not clear, however, precisely how her group could fit her criteria for schizoid personality disorder without any of the above problems. Her criteria include "emotional detachment" and "rigidity, sometimes to the point of obsession", and she describes the children as using odd "metaphorical" language. As before, the terms are too vague to allow a principled distinction to be made. The difference between the groups, then, appears to revolve around severity and age of onset – two factors which are intimately connected (since milder impairments take longer to reach parents' attention), and which provide no evidence of qualitative rather than quantitative differences.

It is hard to see anything in the diagnostic criteria which Wolff & Cull (1986) propose for the disorder, which could in principle distinguish schizoid personality disorder from autism (at the higher-ability end of the spectrum). They list six core features of schizoid personality disorder, as follows:

1. solitariness;
2. impaired empathy and emotional detachment;
3. increased sensitivity, amounting to paranoia;
4. unusual styles of communication;
5. rigidity of mental set, e.g. single-minded pursuit of special interests.

Only "increased sensitivity" would look out of place in a description of an able autistic child. Wolff & Cull claim that Asperger's syndrome is a severe form of schizoid personality disorder, the latter being a broader category covering cases not fitting Asperger's syndrome criteria, and overlapping with ICD–9's "schizoid paranoid personality disorder". An important question, then, is how the schizoid personality disorder children who *do not* have Asperger's syndrome differ from those who *do*? This is not made clear, and the implication is once again that the difference is in severity.

Nagy & Szatmari (1986) claim that Asperger's, Wing's and Wolff's descriptions all refer to the same population of children, which corresponds to DSM–III "schizoid personality disorder". However, this diagnosis includes ideas of reference and abnormal perceptual experiences as features, and does not mention problems with non-verbal expression – a feature which some researchers (e.g. Tantam 1988c) believe to be of primary importance in Asperger's syndrome. Such a diagnosis underestimates the importance of the odd speech, special interests and deficits in non-verbal communication shown by those with Asperger's syndrome. As such, it is unlikely to aid in the provision of the right schooling and care for this group. As Wing (1984) says, while making links between Asperger's syndrome and autism has useful implications for management, a diagnosis of schizoid personality disorder may be "distressing without being constructive". She also makes the important point that the latter diagnosis is as yet vague and, while it may include some people with Asperger's syndrome, also includes many with quite different disorders.

Distinguishing diagnoses

A large number of syndromes similar to autism have been suggested and given different names. Which of these fall within the autistic spectrum (differing only in degree of impairment), and which represent distinct disorders (different in the nature of the underlying impairment), is as yet unclear. Of course, such judgements will depend greatly on the nature of our psychological theories of autism. For example, if a theory of autism posits that the fundamental and defining handicap leads to communication, socialization, and imagination impairments, then a child who shows flexible and creative make-believe play cannot be said to be autistic. On the other hand, a child who shows subtle (but characteristic) pragmatic impairments, rather than the more typical gross deficits, could still be diagnosed autistic, without stretching the diagnostic boundaries past usefulness. As Wing & Gould (1979) have shown, an autistic person may demonstrate social incompetence just as much in an active but odd attempt to make friends as in avoiding all human contact. In some sense, then, our answers to the question "What is autism?", at the three levels of explanation, will inform our judgements about related disorders which are *not* autism.

Can autism be cured?

At the present time there is sadly no cure for autism, although there are many treatments and therapies available. Biological treatments are sometimes used, although no drug has been found to date which is effective in helping all people with autism, and at best drug treatments reduce anxiety and improve behaviour – they do not take away the individual's autism. Fenfluramine (which reduces levels of serotonin in the blood), megavitamins (in particular B_6 with magnesium) and naltrexone (which blocks opioids in the brain) have all been claimed to help some individuals.

Behavioural therapies, and in particular educational systems with insightful and dedicated teachers, can have an enormous impact on individuals with autism – reducing problem behaviours, teaching coping skills and maximizing potential by concentrating on assets and talents. In terms of the three levels discussed in Chapter 1, autistic behaviour can be changed, but the core biological and cognitive deficits cannot at present be cured.

Therapies: how to assess "miracle cures"

Throughout the history of autism, there have been claims for miraculous cures, which raise the hopes of parents, but which fade under scrutiny and are soon forgotten. Such is the speed with which these therapies come and go, that it would not be useful here to discuss specific current therapies – any such discussion would soon be out of date. Instead, this section will suggest some criteria for assessing therapies, which are applicable to any new intervention, and which should help you to make up your own mind about claims of miracle cures.

Assessment should be independent, since the teacher or parent administering the therapy may have such faith in the treatment that they cannot be impartial. So, for example, in drug trials, it is important that those measuring the effects are "blind" to whether the subject has or has not received the drug. An outsider should assess the child and, where possible, this should be done with standardized instruments rather than simply by subjective judgement. Instruments which may be useful include IQ tests such as the Weschler Intelligence Scale for Children – Revised (WISC–R) and the Weschler Adult Intelligence Scale (WAIS) (Wechsler 1974, 1981), measures of autistic behaviour such as the Childhood Autism Rating Scale (Schopler et al. 1980), and measures of daily-life competence such as the Vineland Adaptive Behaviour Scales (Sparrow et al. 1984).

Before and after a therapy is used the child's level of functioning (including their diagnostic status) must be assessed (preferably with an objective measure). Measurement before therapy begins establishes a baseline. After some period of therapy, the child should be reassessed, if possible with the same instrument, to estimate gains. In some cases it is also useful to see how much of the benefit is permanent and how much is reversible and dependent on the child remaining within the therapy. So, for example, in assessing the effects of therapeutic drugs, the child's functioning before taking the drug is measured, followed by testing while he has been on the drug for a while, and finally the child's functioning when once again off the drug is measured. This measurement of treatment gains after therapy is completed may be particularly important for children in a therapy which is not available throughout the lifetime into adulthood.

Controls are a vital part of the experimental validation of a therapeutic regime. Most children with autism make some progress as they grow older, whatever the provision made for them. So it is important to assess any gains made in a specific therapy against gains that could be expected anyway. In other words the specific therapeutic effects of an intervention can only be assessed against a picture of continuing development. This is clearly very hard, since it is impossible to know how a child would have developed had he not received a therapy which he has undergone. The normal approach would be to compare a child in the therapy with a similar child who did not receive a specific intervention of that type. With autistic children, who often seem so very different from one another, it may be hard to find an appropriate "control" against which to compare progress. Bases for matching may include intellectual level (IQ) or mental age, chronological age, severity of disorder, schooling type and sex. If no single child can be found to provide a good comparison and control, a group of children can be used, and their characteristics taken on average as control data.

Anyone who has really found a cure for autism, and those who have discovered a worthwhile intervention, should be happy to have their efforts assessed in this thorough fashion, and should be open to visits by unbiased outsiders. The criteria above are also useful for assessing an individual's gains under a particular teaching programme, and could be used by a teacher to guide measurement of how different pupils are progressing under different teaching strategies.

Conclusions

Autism is a disorder which fascinates because it seems to be so essentially a disorder of the human condition. It is hard to imagine an adequate animal model of the complex pattern of assets and deficits shown by individu-

111

als with autism. Autism is a human disorder which offers us a glimpse of experience close to, and yet perhaps infinitely far from, our own perception of ourselves and our social world. Are we all "a bit autistic"? Does autism merge into the continuum of normality? These are questions which fascinate all those who know about autism. This chapter has explored the possible borderlands of autism. The next, and final, chapter looks to the future, and describes one theory of autism which may have new implications for our understanding of the relations between what is "normal" and what is "autistic".

Suggested reading

Brook, S. L. & D. M. Bowler 1992. Autism by another name? Semantic and pragmatic impairments in children. *Journal of Autism and Developmental Disorders* **22**, 61–81.

Semrud-Clikeman, M. & G. W. Hynd 1990. Right hemisphere dysfunction in nonverbal learning disabilities: social, academic and adaptive functioning in adults and children. *Psychological Bulletin* **107**, 196–209.

Wolff, S. 1991. Schizoid personality in childhood and adult life. I: the vagaries of diagnostic labelling. *British Journal of Psychiatry* **159**, 615–20.

Chapter 10

Remaining puzzles: a look to the future

Taking stock

This book has reviewed current work on the nature of autism at the biological, behavioural and cognitive levels. It has dealt, in particular, with current understanding of the autistic child's mind – psychological theories of autism. One theory, the idea that people with autism can be characterized as suffering from a type of "mind-blindness", has been particularly influential in recent years. This theory has been useful to the study of child development in general – not because it is necessarily correct (that is still debatable) – but because it is a *causal* account which is both *specific* and *falsifiable*. The theory of mind account of autism has focused on the critical triad of impairments (Wing & Gould 1979) in socialization, communication and imagination. Not only has it helped to make sense of this triad, it has also allowed us to make "fine cuts" *within* the triad of autistic impairments. Thus, the mentalizing-deficit account has allowed a systematic approach to the impaired and unimpaired social and communicative behaviour of people with autism (see Tables 10.1 & 10.2), using a "fine cuts" technique which aims to pit two behaviours against each other which differ only in the demands they make upon the ability to mentalize. This approach suits the current climate of increased interest in the modular nature of mental capacities (e.g. Fodor 1983, Cosmides 1989). It has allowed us to think about social and communicative behaviour in a new way, and, for this reason, autism has come to be a test case for many theories of normal development (e.g. Sperber & Wilson's 1986 relevance theory, Happé 1993).

Table 10.1 Autistic assets and deficits, as predicted by the "fine cuts" technique, between tasks which require mentalizing and those which do not.

Assets	Deficits
ordering behavioural pictures (Baron-Cohen et al. 1986)	ordering mentalistic pictures
understanding "see" (Perner et al. 1989)	understanding "know"
protoimperative pointing (Baron-Cohen 1989c)	protodeclarative pointing
sabotage (Sodian & Frith 1992)	deception
false photographs (Leekam & Perner 1991, Leslie & Thaiss 1992)	false beliefs
recognising happiness and sadness (Baron-Cohen et al. 1993a)	recognizing surprise
object occlusion (Baron-Cohen 1992)	information occlusion
literal expression (Happé 1993)	metaphorical expression

Table 10.2 Autistic assets and deficits observed in real life.

Assets	Deficits
elicited structured play (Wetherby & Prutting 1984)	spontaneous pretend play
instrumental gestures (Attwood et al. 1988)	expressive gestures
talking about desires and emotions (Tager-Flusberg 1993)	talking about beliefs and ideas
using person as tool (Phillips 1993)	using person as receiver of information
showing "active" sociability (Frith et al. 1994)	showing "interactive" sociability

Looking beyond theory of mind

Just how well does the theory of mind account explain autism? The "mind-blindness" theory has helped us to understand the nature of the autistic child's impairments in play, social interaction and verbal and nonverbal communication. But there is more to autism than the classic triad of impairments. Just as the mentalizing deficit theory of autism cannot explain all *people* with autism (see Ch. 7), so it cannot explain all *features* of autism.

Non-triad features

Clinical impressions, originating with Kanner (1943) and Asperger (1944, translated in Frith 1991b), and withstanding the test of time, include the following:

- restricted repertoire of interests (necessary for diagnosis in DSM–III–R, American Psychiatric Association 1987);
- obsessive desire for sameness (one of two cardinal features for Kanner & Eisenberg 1956);
- islets of ability (an essential criterion in Kanner 1943);
- idiot savant abilities (striking in 1 in 10 autistic children, Rimland 1978);
- excellent rote memory (emphasized by Kanner 1943);
- preoccupation with parts of objects (a diagnostic feature in the forthcoming DSM–IV).

All of these non-triad aspects of autism are vividly documented in the many parental accounts of the development of autistic children (Park 1987, Hart 1989, McDonnell 1993). None of these aspects can be well explained by a lack of mentalizing.

Of course, clinically striking features shown by people with autism need not be specific features of the disorder. However, there is also a substantial body of experimental work, much of it predating the mentalizing theory, which demonstrates non-social abnormalities which are specific to autism. Hermelin & O'Connor were the first to introduce what was, in effect, a different "fine cuts" method (summarized in their 1970 monograph) – namely the comparison of closely matched groups of autistic and non-autistic handicapped children of the same mental age. Table 10.3 summarizes some of the relevant findings.

115

Table 10.3 Experimental findings not accounted for by mind-blindness. Surprising advantages and disadvantages on cognitive tasks, shown by autistic subjects relative to normally expected asymmetries.

Unusual strength	Unusual weakness
memory for word strings (Hermelin & O'Connor 1967)	memory for sentences
memory for unrelated items (Tager-Flusberg 1991)	memory for related items
echoing nonsense (Aurnhammer-Frith 1969)	echoing with repair
pattern imposition (Frith 1970ab)	pattern detection
jigsaw by shape (Frith & Hermelin 1969)	jigsaw by picture
sorting faces by accessories (Weeks & Hobson 1987)	sorting faces by emotion
recognizing faces upside-down (Langdell 1978)	recognising faces right-way-up

The central coherence theory

Motivated by the strong belief that both the assets and the deficits of autism spring from a single cause at the cognitive level, Frith (1989a) proposed that autism is characterized by a specific imbalance in integration of information at different levels. A characteristic of *normal* information-processing appears to be the tendency to draw together diverse information to construct higher-level meaning in context – *"central coherence"* in Frith's words. For example, the gist of a story is easily recalled, while the actual surface form is quickly lost, and is effortful to retain. Bartlett (1932), summarizing his famous series of experiments on remembering images and stories, concluded: "an individual does not normally take [such] a situation detail by detail . . . In all ordinary instances he has an overmastering tendency simply to get a general impression of the whole; and, on the basis of this, he constructs the probable detail". Another instance of central coherence is the ease with which we recognize the contextually-appropriate sense of the many ambiguous words used in everyday speech (son–sun, meet–meat, sew–so, pear–pair). A similar tendency to process information in context for global meaning is seen with non-verbal material – for example, our common tendency to misinterpret details in a jigsaw piece according to the expected position in the whole picture. It is likely that this preference for higher levels of meaning may characterize even mentally handicapped (non-autistic) individuals – who appear to be sensitive to the advantage of recalling organized versus jumbled material (e.g. Hermelin & O'Connor 1967).

Frith suggested that this universal feature of human information processing is disturbed in autism, and that a lack of central coherence could explain very parsimoniously the assets and deficits, shown in Table 10.3. Perhaps the easiest way in which to convey the idea of weak central coherence is through a clinical anecdote (Fig. 10.1):

> A clinician testing a bright autistic boy presented him with a toy bed, and asked the child to name the parts. The child correctly labelled the bed, mattress and quilt. The clinician then pointed to the pillow and asked, "And what is this?" The boy replied, "It's a piece of ravioli".

The child in the anecdote was not joking, nor was his sight impaired – indeed the clinician commented that the pillow did indeed look like a piece of ravioli, *if taken out of context*. However, normal subjects appear to be constrained in their interpretation of information by the context in which stimuli are presented (e.g. Palmer 1975). The central coherence theory suggests that autistic subjects are peculiarly free from such contextual constraints.

On the basis of the theory that people with autism have weak central coherence, Frith predicted that autistic subjects would be relatively good at tasks where attention to local information – relatively piecemeal processing – is advantageous, but poor at tasks requiring the recognition of global meaning.

Empirical evidence: assets

A first striking signpost towards the theory appeared quite unexpectedly, when Amitta Shah set off to look at autistic children's putative perceptual impairments on the Embedded Figures Test. She found that the children were almost better than the experimenter! Subjects with autism were compared with learning disabled children of the same age and mental age, and with normal 9-year-olds. The children were given the Children's Embed-

Figure 10.1 A clinical example of weak coherence (by kind permission of the artist, Axel Scheffler).

ded Figures Test (CEFT, Witkin et al. 1971), a test which involves spotting a hidden figure (triangle or house shape) among a larger meaningful drawing (e.g. a clock). Out of a maximum score of 25, autistic children got a mean of 21 items correct, while the two control groups (which did not differ significantly in their scores) achieved 15 or less. Gottschaldt (1926) ascribed the difficulty of finding embedded figures to the overwhelming "predominance of the whole". The ease and speed with which autistic subjects picked out the hidden figure in Shah & Frith's (1983) study was reminiscent of their rapid style of locating tiny objects (e.g. a thread on a patterned carpet) and their immediate discovery of minute changes in familiar layouts (e.g. the arrangement of cleaning materials on a bathroom shelf), as often described anecdotally.

The study of embedded figures was introduced into experimental psychology by the Gestalt psychologists, who believed that an effort was needed to resist the tendency to see the forcefully-created Gestalt or whole, at the expense of the constituent parts (Koffka 1935). Perhaps, this struggle to resist overall gestalt forces does not occur for autistic subjects. If people with autism, due to weak central coherence, have privileged access to the parts and details normally securely embedded in whole figures, then novel predictions can be made about the nature of their islets of ability.

The *Block Design* subtest of the Wechsler Intelligence Scales (Wechsler 1974, 1981) is consistently found to be a test on which autistic people show superior performance relative to other subtests, and often relative to other people of the same age. This test, first introduced by Kohs (1923), requires the breaking up of line drawings into logical units, so that individual blocks can be used to reconstruct the original design from its separate parts. The designs are notable for their strong Gestalt qualities, and the difficulty which most people experience with this task appears to relate to problems in breaking up the whole design into the constituent blocks. While many authors have recognized this subtest as an islet of ability in autism, this fact has generally been explained as due to intact or superior general spatial skills (Lockyer & Rutter 1970, Prior 1979). Shah & Frith (1993) suggested, on the basis of the central coherence theory, that the advantage shown by autistic subjects is due specifically to their ability to see parts over wholes. They predicted that normal, but not autistic, subjects would benefit from pre-segmentation of the designs.

Shah & Frith (1993) tested subjects with autism, subjects with learning difficulties (mental handicap), and normal 10- and 16-year-olds with 40 different block designs which had to be constructed from either whole or presegmented drawn models (Fig. 10.2). The results showed that the autistic subjects' skill on this task resulted from a greater ability to segment the design. Autistic subjects showed superior performance compared to controls in one condition only – when working from whole designs. The great

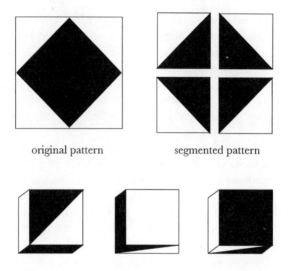

original pattern   segmented pattern

types of blocks available for making the pattern

Figure 10.2 Examples of the materials used in Shah & Frith's (1993) Block Design task (reprinted from Frith 1989a).

advantage which the control subjects gained from using pre-segmented designs was significantly diminished in the autistic subjects, regardless of their IQ level.

Empirical evidence: deficits

While weak central coherence confers significant advantages in tasks where preferential processing of parts over wholes is useful, it would be expected to confer marked disadvantages in tasks which involve interpretation of individual stimuli in terms of overall context and meaning. An interesting example is the processing of faces, which seems to involve both featural (part) and configural (whole) processing (Tanaka & Farah 1993). Of these two types of information, it appears to be configural processing which is disrupted by the inverted presentation of faces (Bartlett & Searcy 1993, Rhodes et al. 1993). This may explain the previously puzzling finding that autistic subjects show a diminished disadvantage in processing inverted faces (Langdell 1978, Hobson et al. 1988).

One case in which the meaning of individual stimuli is changed by their context is in the disambiguation of homographs. In order to choose the correct (context-appropriate) pronunciation in the following sentences, one must process the final word as part of the whole sentence meaning: "He had a pink *bow*", "He made a deep *bow*". Frith & Snowling (1983) predicted that this sort of contextual disambiguation would be problematic for people with autism. They compared children with autism, dyslexic children and normal children of the same reading age. The number of words read with the contextually-appropriate pronunciation ranged from 5 to 7 out of 10 for the autistic children, who tended to give the more frequent pronunciation regardless of sentence context. By contrast, the normal and dyslexic children read between 7 and 9 of the 10 homographs in a contextually-determined manner. This finding suggests that autistic children, although excellent at decoding single words, tend not to integrate meaning across a sentence to allow context-dependent processing of ambiguous information. Figure 10.3 illustrates this piecemeal processing style, which would leave the autistic reader with little idea as to the correct pronunciation of the homograph target word. Frith & Snowling's results fit well with previous findings (Table 10.3) concerning failure to use meaning and redundancy in memory tasks. In addition, the results of this reading study call to mind Kanner's (1943) own description of his original cases: "the children read monotonously, and a story . . . is experienced in unrelated portions rather than in its coherent totality".

The abnormality of excellence

The hypothesis that people with autism show weak central coherence aims to explain both the glaring impairments and the outstanding skills of autism as resulting from a single characteristic of information processing. One characteristic of this theory is that it claims that the islets of ability and savant skills (mentioned in Ch. 3) are achieved through relatively abnormal processing, and predicts that this may be revealed in abnormal error patterns. One example might be the type of error made in the Block Design test. The central coherence theory suggests that, where errors are made at all on Block Design, these will be errors which violate the overall pattern, rather than the details. Kramer et al. (1991) found that in normal adult subjects there was a strong relation between the number of such configuration-breaking errors made on the Block Design test and the number of local (versus global) choices made in a similarity-judgement task (Kimchi

Mary   took   the dog   for a walk.

She   went   to fetch   the lead.

Figure 10.3 Illustration of a piecemeal approach in the homograph reading task (by kind permission of the artist, Axel Scheffler).

& Palmer 1982). Preliminary data from subjects with autism (Happé, 1994d) suggest that, in contrast to normal children, errors violating configuration are far more common than errors violating pattern details in autistic Block Design performance.

A second example concerns idiot savant drawing ability. Excellent drawing ability may be characterized by a relatively piecemeal drawing style. Mottron & Belleville (1993) found, in a case study of one autistic man with exceptional artistic ability, that performance on three different tasks suggested an anomaly in the hierarchical organization of the local and global parts of figures. The authors observed that the subject "began his drawing by a secondary detail and then progressed by adding contiguous elements", and concluded that his drawings showed "no privileged status of the global form . . . but rather a construction by local progression". In contrast, a professional draughtsman who acted as a control started by constructing outlines and then proceeded to parts. It remains to be seen whether other savant abilities can be explained in terms of a similarly local and detail-observant processing style.

Central coherence and mentalizing

Central coherence may be helpful in explaining some of the real-life features that have so far resisted explanation, as well as making sense of a body of experimental work not well accounted for by the mentalizing deficit theory. Can it also shed light on the continuing handicaps of those talented autistic subjects who show consistent evidence of some mentalizing ability (see Ch. 7)? Recently, I have attempted to explore the links between central coherence and theory of mind, using Snowling & Frith's (1986) homograph reading task (Happé 1991b). Autistic subjects were tested on a battery of theory of mind tasks at two levels of difficulty (first- and second-order theory of mind), and grouped according to their performance (Happé 1993, 1994a). Five subjects who failed all the theory of mind tasks, five subjects who passed all and only first-order tasks, and six subjects who passed both first- and second-order theory of mind tasks were compared with 14 subjects aged 7–8 years. The autistic subjects were of mean age 18 years, and had a mean IQ of around 80. The three autistic groups and the control group obtained the same score for total number of words correctly read. As predicted, however, the young normal subjects, but not the autistic subjects, were sensitive to the relative position of target homograph and disambiguating context (e.g. "There was a big tear in her eye", versus "In her dress there was a big tear"). The normal controls showed a significant advantage when sentence context occurred before target words (scoring 5 out of 5, versus 2 out of 5 where target came first), while the autistic subjects (as in

Frith & Snowling 1983) tended to give the more frequent pronunciation regardless (3 out of 5 appropriate pronunciations in each case). The important point of this study was that this was true of all three autistic groups, irrespective of level of theory of mind performance. Even those subjects who consistently passed all the theory of mind tasks (mean verbal IQ 90) failed to use sentence context to disambiguate homograph pronunciation. It is possible, therefore, to think of weak central coherence as a characteristic of even those autistic subjects who possess some mentalizing ability.

I have explored this preliminary idea further by looking at WISC–R and WAIS subtest profiles (Happé 1994e). Thirty children and adults with autism who failed standard first-order false belief tasks were compared with 21 subjects who passed. In both groups, the majority of subjects performed better on the Block Design subtest than on the non-verbal subtests as a whole; for 85 per cent of "failers" and 86 per cent of "passers" the Block Design standard score was higher than own mean non-verbal score. In contrast, performance on the Comprehension subtest (commonly thought to require pragmatic and social skill) was a low point in verbal performance for 76 per cent of "failers" but only 30 per cent of "passers". It seems, then, that while social reasoning difficulties (as shown by Wechsler tests) are striking only in those subjects who fail theory of mind tasks, skill on non-verbal tasks benefitting from weak central coherence is characteristic of both "passers" and "failers".

There is, then, preliminary evidence to suggest that the central coherence hypothesis is a good candidate for explaining the persisting handicaps of the talented minority. So, for example, when theory of mind questions were embedded in slightly more naturalistic tasks, involving extracting information from a story context, even autistic subjects who passed standard second-order false belief tasks showed characteristic and striking errors of mental state attribution (see Ch. 7). It may be that a theory of mind mechanism which is not fed by rich and integrated contextual information is of little use in everyday life.

The finding that weak central coherence appears to characterize autistic people at all levels of theory of mind ability goes against Frith's (1989a) original suggestion that a weakness in central coherence could by itself account for mentalizing impairments. At present, all the evidence suggests that we should retain the idea of a modular and specific mentalizing deficit in our causal explanation of the triad of impairments in autism. Nevertheless, for a full understanding of autism in all its forms, this explanation alone will not suffice. Therefore, an exciting suggestion is that there may

124

be two rather different cognitive characteristics that underlie autism.

Leslie (1987, 1988) has suggested that the mentalizing deficit can be usefully conceptualized as the impairment of a single modular system. This system has a neurological basis – which may be damaged leaving other functions intact (e.g. normal IQ). The ability to mentalize would appear to be of such evolutionary value (Byrne & Whiten 1988, Whiten 1991) that only insult to the brain can produce deficits in this area. Of course normal individuals vary in their social competence, but this continuum at the behavioural level is unlikely to be due to individual differences in the basic ability to "know that we know".

By contrast, the processing characteristic of weak central coherence, as illustrated above, gives both advantages and disadvantages, as would strong central coherence. It is possible, then, to think of this balance (between preference for parts versus wholes) as akin to a cognitive style, which may vary in the normal population. The wide range of scores commonly attained in normal samples on the Embedded Figures Test and Wechsler Block Design subtest supports this idea. No doubt, this style would be subject to environmental influences, but, in addition, it may have a genetic component (Goodenough et al. 1977). It may be interesting, then, to focus on the strengths and weaknesses of autistic children's processing, in terms of weak central coherence, in looking for the extended phenotype of autism. Some initial evidence for this may be found in the report by Landa et al. (1991) that the parents of children with autism tell rather less coherent spontaneous narratives than do controls.

Central coherence and executive function

With its speculative link to cognitive style, rather than straightforward deficit, the central coherence hypothesis differs radically not only from the theory of mind account, but also from other recent theories of autism. In fact, every other current psychological theory (see Ch. 6) claims that some significant and objectively harmful deficit is primary in autism. Perhaps the most influential of such general theories is the idea that autistic people have executive function deficits, which in turn cause social and non-social abnormalities. The umbrella term "executive functions" covers a multitude of higher cognitive capacities, and so is likely to overlap to some degree with conceptions both of central coherence and of theory of mind. However, the hypothesis that autistic people have relatively weak central coherence makes specific and distinct predictions even within the area of executive function. For example, the executive component "inhibition of prepotent but incorrect responses" may contain two separable elements: inhibition, and the recognition of context-appropriate response. One factor which can make a prepotent response incorrect is a change of context. If a stimulus is treated in the same way regardless of context, this may look like a failure of inhibition. However, autistic people may have no problem in inhibiting action where context is irrelevant. Of course it may be that some people with autism do have an additional impairment in inhibitory control, just as some have peripheral perceptual handicaps or specific language problems.

Future prospects

The central coherence account of autism is clearly still tentative and suffers from a certain degree of over-extension. It is not clear where the limits of this theory should be drawn – it is perhaps in danger of trying to take on the whole problem of "meaning"! One of the areas for future definition will be the *level* at which coherence is weak in autism. While Block Design and Embedded Figures tests appear to tap processing characteristics at a fairly low or perceptual level, work on memory and verbal comprehension suggests higher-level coherence deficits. Coherence can be seen at many levels in normal subjects, from the global precedence effect in perception of hierarchical figures (Navon 1977) to the synthesis of large amounts of information and extraction of inferences in narrative processing (e.g. Trabasso & Suh 1993). One interesting way forward may be to contrast local coherence within modular systems, and global coherence across these systems in central processing. So, for example, the calendrical calculating skills of some people with autism (Hermelin & O'Connor 1986) clearly show that information within a restricted domain can be integrated and processed together, but the failure of many such savants to apply these numerical skills more widely (some cannot multiply two given numbers) suggests a modular system specialized for a very narrow cognitive task. Similarly, Norris (1990) found that his attempts to build a connectionist model of an "idiot savant date calculator" only succeeded when forced to take a modular approach.

Level of coherence may be relative. So, for example, within text there is the word-to-word effect of local association, the effect of sentence context, and the larger effect of story structure. These three levels may be dissociable, and it may be that people with autism process the most local of the levels available in open-ended tasks. The importance of testing central coherence with open-ended tasks is suggested by a number of findings. For example, Snowling & Frith (1986) demonstrated that it was possible to train subjects with autism to give the context-appropriate (but less frequent) pronunciation of ambiguous homographs. Weeks & Hobson (1987) found that autistic subjects sorted photographs of faces by type of hat when given a free choice, but were able, when asked, to sort again taking into account facial expressions. It seems likely, then, that autistic weak central coherence is most clearly shown as a (non-conscious) processing preference, which may reflect the relative cost of two types of processing (relatively global and meaningful versus relatively local and piecemeal).

The central coherence hypothesis draws into focus many features of autism which have been neglected in recent investigations of the autistic social handicap. So, for example, while Wing's triad of impairments in socialization, imagination and communication has been much discussed in the recent literature, far less attention has been given to a later analysis of the "central core of the problem" in autism, in which Wing (1981b) outlined three rather different points. While Wing (1981b) mentions as core problems both impairment in communication and failure to recognize "human beings as different from other features of the environment" (handicaps which would follow from a lack of theory of mind), she gives as the third area of handicap the failure to "seek out experiences and make a coherent story out of them". This feature of autism would appear to be well accounted for in terms of a deficit in central coherence. Some of Kanner's observations, too, fit well the idea of an autistic impairment in drawing together information for processing of meaning in context. Kanner (1943) was struck by the excellent rote memory skills of his patients, and, in particular, by the lack of meaning in what the children memorized: "To a child two or three years old, all these words, numbers and poems ('Questions and answers of the Presbyterian Catechism'; 'Mendelssohn's violin concertos'; the 'Twenty-third Psalm'; a French lullaby; an encyclopedia index page) could hardly have more meaning than sets of nonsense syllables to adults". Kanner also comments on the tendency for fragmentary processing, and its rôle in the children's resistance to change: "a situation, a performance, a sentence is not regarded as complete if it is not made up of exactly the same elements that were present at the time the child was first confronted with it". Kanner saw as a universal feature of autism the "inability to experience wholes without full attention to the constituent parts", a char-

127

acteristic that would follow from a deficit in central coherence.

Just as the idea of a deficit in theory of mind has taken several years and considerable (and continuing) work to be empirically established, so the idea of a weakness in central coherence will require a systematic programme of research. Like the theory of mind account, it is to be hoped that, whether right or wrong, the central coherence theory will form a useful framework for thinking about autism in the future.

Conclusions

In Chapter 2 two folktales were given, with the suggestion that such stories may be records of awareness of autism in the community from the earliest times. It seems fitting, then, to end with another folktale which may have relevance for autism. The following story, told through generations by the Ashanti people of West Africa, may be read as a parable of the value of the autistic view of the world; a son outcast because of his strange behaviour, saves the day precisely because of his idiosyncratic "insistence on sameness".

How the foolish son defeated Death

There was once a woman of Nyankumase who had three sons. Two of the boys were very clever, and as they grew older they married well and became wealthy citizens so that their mother was very proud of them.

The third son, who was called Akyene, was regarded by all as a fool. From a small boy he had been bullied in the house, he had been punished for all his mistakes and generally made miserable. He never seemed to have any ambition or to do anything useful. So the mother, who loved her two elder sons dearly, became ashamed of the youngest. Life at home became so unhappy for him that, at last . . . he went to live by himself in the forest.

There, in the forest, he built himself a small hut. Nearby, he made a big playground and covered its surface in fine sand. He would play for hours, happily dancing or making patterns in the sand.

One day it happened that Death came to take away the woman. The two older brothers offered him all their riches if only he would leave them their mother. But all was not enough, and Death insisted on taking her away.

As Death and the woman went on their way, she thought of her youngest son, and begged that she might pass by his hut in the forest and say farewell to him.

Death knew the foolish son and did not fear him, so he let the woman stop and call Akyene.

When Akyene came up to them, Death said: "I am taking your mother away, Akyene, what can you do to save her?" and he laughed.

Akyene replied: "I have nothing to give, friend Death, but you have walked all over my playground and made a mess of it. Before you go you must cover all the footmarks and then, and only then, you can take my mother away." . . . Death, in the forest, started to cover up his footsteps. He made the ground smooth over them and thought he would soon be finished. But Akyene and his mother sat and watched. No sooner had he covered one set of footsteps than another appeared, and in his anger he made yet more. At last, he was quite exhausted and sat down to mop his brow.

"Take your mother," he said to Akyene. "I underestimated your intelligence." . . . And he stumped off through the forest leaving Akyene his mother.

Akyene's mother embraced him warmly and begged his forgiveness for the way she had treated him in the past. Then they went hand in hand back to the village . . .

The people were amazed. The two rich sons drew back in wonder and demanded to know who had freed her. "Are you a ghost?" they asked. "Indeed no!" she replied. "I have been saved by Akyene whom I thought a fool."

Then the funeral was turned to rejoicing, and the two rich sons begged their brother's forgiveness and gave him the place of honour.

As for Akyene, he returned home again and lived in honour and happiness. His mother was ashamed of her lack of understanding and cared for him tenderly until he found a wife. She realized at last that it is bad to cast away even a foolish son, because was it not Akyene, the fool, who saved her from Death?

(From *The pineapple child and other tales of the Ashanti*, Appiah 1969)

Bibliography

Aarons, M. & T. Gittens 1991. *The handbook of autism*. London: Tavistock/Routledge.

Adams, C. & D. V. M. Bishop 1989. Conversational characteristics of children with semantic–pragmatic disorder. I: Exchange structure, turntaking, repairs and cohesion. *British Journal of Disorders of Communication* **24**, 211–39.

Adrien, J. L., M. Faure, A. Perrot, L. Hameury, B. Garrau, C. Barthelemy, D. Savage 1991. Autism and family home movies: preliminary findings. *Journal of Autism and Developmental Disorders* **21**, 43–51.

Aitken, K. 1991. Annotation: examining the evidence for a common structural basis to autism. *Developmental Medicine and Child Neurology* **33**, 930–38.

American Psychiatric Association 1980. *Diagnostic and statistical manual of mental disorders*, 3rd edn. Washington, DC: American Psychiatric Association.

American Psychiatric Association 1987. *Diagnostic and statistical manual of mental disorders*, 3rd revised edn. Washington, DC: American Psychiatric Association.

Appiah, P. (ed.) 1969. *The pineapple child and other tales from the Ashanti*. London: André Deutsch.

Asperger, H. 1944. Die "Autistischen Psychopathen" im Kindesalter. *Archiv für Psychiatrie und Nervenkrankheiten* **117**, 76–136.

Asperger, H. 1979. Problems of infantile autism. *Communication* **13**, 45–52.

Astington, J. W. & A. Gopnik 1991. Theoretical explanations of children's understanding of the mind. *British Journal of Developmental Psychology* **9**, 7–31.

Attwood, A. H., U. Frith, B. Hermelin 1988. The understanding and use of interpersonal gestures by autistic and Down's syndrome children. *Journal of Autism and Developmental Disorders* **18**, 241–57.

August, G. J., M. A. Stewart, L. Tsai 1981. The incidence of cognitive disabilities in the siblings of autistic children. *British Journal of Psychiatry* **138**, 416–22.

Aurnhammer-Frith, U. 1969. Emphasis and meaning in recall in normal and autistic children. *Language and Speech* **12**, 29–38.

Avis, J. & P. L. Harris 1991. Belief–desire reasoning among Baka children: evidence for a universal conception of mind. *Child Development* **62**, 460–7.

Ballotin, U., M. Bejor, A. Cecchini, A. Martelli, S. Palazzi, G. Lanzi 1989. Infantile autism and computerized tomography brain-scan findings: specific versus nonspecific abnormalities. *Journal of Autism and Developmental Disorders* **19**, 109–17.

Baltaxe, C. A. M. 1977. Pragmatic deficits in the language of autistic adolescents. *Journal of Pediatric Psychology* **2**, 176–80.

Baron-Cohen, S. 1989a. The autistic child's theory of mind: a case of specific developmental delay. *Journal of Child Psychology and Psychiatry* **30**, 285–97.

Baron-Cohen, S. 1989b. Perceptual rôle taking and protodeclarative pointing in autism. *British Journal of Developmental Psychology* **7**, 113–27.

Baron-Cohen, S. 1989c. Are autistic children behaviourists? An examination of their mental–physical and appearance–reality distinctions. *Journal of Autism and Developmental Disorders* **19**, 579–600.

Baron-Cohen, S. 1991. Do people with autism understand what causes emotion? *Child Development* **62**, 385–95.

Baron-Cohen, S. 1992. Out of sight or out of mind? Another look at deception in autism. *Journal of Child Psychology and Psychiatry* **33**, 1141–55.

Baron-Cohen, S. 1994. How to build a baby that can read minds: cognitive mechanisms in mindreading. *Cahiers de Psychologie Cognitive*, **13**, in press.

Baron-Cohen, S. & P. Bolton 1993. *Autism: the facts*. Oxford: Oxford University Press.

Baron-Cohen, S., A. M. Leslie, U. Frith 1985. Does the autistic child have a "theory of mind"? *Cognition* **21**, 37–46.

Baron-Cohen, S., A. M. Leslie, U. Frith 1986. Mechanical, behavioural and intentional understanding of picture stories in autistic children. *British Journal of Developmental Psychology* **4**, 113–25.

Baron-Cohen, S., J. Allen, C. Gillberg 1992. Can autism be detected at 18 months? The needle, the haystack, and the CHAT. *British Journal of Psychiatry* **161**, 839–43.

Baron-Cohen, S., A. Spitz, P. Cross 1993a. Can children with autism recognise surprise? *Cognition and Emotion* **7**, 507–16.

Baron-Cohen, S., H. Tager-Flusberg, D. J. Cohen (eds) 1993b. *Understanding other minds: perspectives from autism*. Oxford: Oxford University Press.

Bartlett, F. C. 1932. *Remembering: a study in experimental and social psychology*. Cambridge, England: Cambridge University Press.

Bartlett, J. C. & J. Searcy 1993. Inversion and configuration of faces. *Cognitive Psychology* **25**, 281–316.

Bauman, M. L. & T. L. Kemper 1985. Histo-anatomic observations of the brain in early infantile autism. *Neurology* **35**, 866–74.

Bettelheim, B. 1956. Childhood schizophrenia as a reaction to extreme situations. *Journal of Orthopsychiatry* **26**, 507–518.

Bettelheim, B. 1967. *The empty fortress: infantile autism and the birth of the self*. New York: The Free Press.

Bishop, D. V. M. 1989. Autism, Asperger's syndrome and semantic–pragmatic disorder: where are the boundaries? *British Journal of Disorders of Communication* **24**, 107–21.

Bishop, D. V. M. 1993. Annotation: autism, executive functions and theory of mind: a neuropsychological perspective. *Journal of Child Psychology and Psychiatry* **34**, 279–93.

Bishop, D. V. M. & C. Adams 1989. Conversational characteristics of children with semantic–pragmatic disorder. II: what features lead to a judgement of inappropriacy? *British Journal of Disorders of Communication* **24**, 241–63.

Bleuler, E. 1908. The prognosis of dementia praecox. The group of schizophrenias. English translation in *The clinical roots of the schizophrenia concept*, J. Cutting & M. Sheperd (eds) (1987). Cambridge: Cambridge University Press.

Blomquist, H. K., M. Bohmna, S. O. Edvinsson, C. Gillberg, K. M. Gustavon, C. Holmgren, J. Wahlstrom 1985. Frequency of the fragile-X syndrome in infantile autism: a Swedish multicentre study. *Clinical Genetics* **27**, 113–17.

Bolton, P. & M. Rutter 1990. Genetic influences in autism. *International Review of Psychiatry*

2, 67–80.

Boucher, J. 1989. The theory of mind hypothesis of autism: explanation, evidence and assessment. *British Journal of Disorders of Communication* **24**, 181–98.

Bowler, D. M. 1992. "Theory of mind" in Asperger's syndrome. *Journal of Child Psychology and Psychiatry* **33**, 877–93.

Bowman, E. P. 1988. Asperger's syndrome and autism: the case for a connection. *British Journal of Psychiatry* **152**, 377–82.

Bretherton, I. & M. Beeghly 1982. Talking about internal states: the acquisition of an explicit theory of mind. *Developmental Psychology* **18**, 906–21.

Brook, S. L. & D. Bowler 1992. Autism by another name? Semantic and pragmatic impairments in children. *Journal of Autism and Developmental Disorders* **22**, 61–81.

Bryson, S. E., B. S. Clark, I. M. Smith 1988. First report of a Canadian epidemiological study of autistic syndromes. *Journal of Child Psychology and Psychiatry* **29**, 433–45.

Burd, L. & J. Kerbeshian 1987. Asperger's syndrome. *British Journal of Psychiatry* **151**, 417.

Burgoine, E. & L. Wing 1983. Identical triplets with Asperger's syndrome. *British Journal of Psychiatry* **143**, 261–5.

Byrne, R. & A. Whiten (eds) 1988. *Machiavellian intelligence: social expertise and the evolution of intellect in monkeys, apes, and humans.* Oxford: Clarendon Press.

Campbell, M., S. Rosenbloom, R. Perry, A. E. George, I. I. Kricheff, L. Anderson, A. M. Small, S. J. Jennings 1982. Computerised axial tomography in young autistic children. *American Journal of Psychiatry* **139**, 510–12.

Charman, T. & S. Baron-Cohen 1992. Understanding drawings and beliefs: a further test of the metarepresentation theory of autism. *Journal of Child Psychology and Psychiatry* **33**, 1105–12.

Ciadella, P. & N. Mamelle 1989. An epidemiological study of infantile autism in a French department (Rhône): a research note. *Journal of Child Psychology and Psychiatry* **30**, 165–75.

Clarke, A. M. & A. D. B. Clarke 1976. Formerly isolated children. In *Early experience: myth and evidence*, A. M. Clarke & A. D. B. Clarke (eds), 27–34. London: Open Books.

Clarke, P. & M. Rutter 1981. Autistic children's responses to structure and interpersonal demands. *Journal of Autism and Developmental Disorders* **11**, 201–17.

Cohen, D., A. Donnellan, R. Paul (eds) 1987. *Handbook of autism and pervasive developmental disorders.* Chichester: John Wiley.

Coleman, M. & C. Gillberg 1985. *The biology of the autistic syndromes.* New York: Praeger.

Cosmides, L. 1989. The logic of social exchange: has natural selection shaped how humans reason? Studies with the Wason selection task. *Cognition* **31**, 187–276.

Courchesne, E., J. R. Hesselink, T. L. Jernigan, R. Yeung-Courchesne 1987. Abnormal neuroanatomy in a nonretarded person with autism: unusual findings with magnetic resonance imaging. *Archives of Neurology* **44**, 335–41.

Courchesne, E., R. Yeung-Courchesne, G. A. Press, J. R. Hesselink, T. L. Jernigan 1988. Hypoplasia of cerebellar vermal lobules VI and VII in autism. *New England Journal of Medicine* **318**, 1349–54.

Creasey, H., J. M. Rumsey, M. Schwartz, R. Duara, J. L. Rapoport, S. I. Rapoport 1986. Brain morphometry in autistic men as measured by volumetric computed tomography. *Archives of Neurology* **43**, 669–72.

Curcio, F. 1978. Sensorimotor functioning and communication in mute autistic children. *Journal of Autism and Childhood Schizophrenia* **8**, 281–91.

Curtiss, S. 1977. *Genie: a psychological study of a modern-day "wild child"*. New York: Academic Press.

Damasio, A. R. & R. G. Maurer 1978. A neurological model for childhood autism. *Archives of Neurology* **35**, 777–86.

Dawson, G. (ed.) 1989. *Autism: nature, diagnosis and treatment*. New York: Guildford Press.

Dawson, G. 1991. A psychobiological perspective on the early socio-emotional development of children with autism. In *Rochester symposium on developmental psychopathology, vol. 3*, D. Cicchetti & S. L. Toth (eds), 207–234. New York: Rochester Press.

Dawson, G. & A. Lewy 1989. Arousal, attention, and the socioemotional impairments of individuals with autism. In *Autism: nature, diagnosis and treatment*, G. Dawson (ed.), 49–74. New York: Guildford Press.

Dawson, G. & F. C. McKissick 1984. Self-recognition in autistic children. *Journal of Autism and Developmental Disorders* **14**, 383–94.

DeGelder, B. 1987. On not having a theory of mind. *Cognition* **27**, 285–90.

DeLeon, M. J., R. J. Muoz, S. E. Pico 1986. Is there a right hemisphere dysfunction in Asperger's syndrome? *British Journal of Psychiatry* **148**, 745–6.

DeLong, G. R. & J. T. Dwyer 1988. Correlation of family history with specific autistic subgroups: Asperger's syndrome and bipolar affective disease. *Journal of Autism and Developmental Disorders* **18**, 593–600.

Denckla, M. B. 1983. The neuropsychology of socio-emotional learning disabilities. *Archives of Neurology* **40** 461–2.

Dennett, D. C. 1978. Beliefs about beliefs. *Behavioral and Brain Sciences* **4**, 568–70.

Duncan, J. 1986. Disorganization of behaviour after frontal lobe damage. *Cognitive Neuropsychology* **33**, 271–90.

Ehlers, S. & C. Gillberg 1993. The epidemiology of Asperger syndrome. A total population study. *Journal of Child Psychology and Psychiatry* **34**, 1327–50.

Eisenberg, L. 1957. The fathers of autistic children. *American Journal of Orthopsychiatry* **27**, 715–24.

Eisenmajer, R. & M. Prior 1991. Cognitive linguistic correlates of "theory of mind" ability in autistic children. *British Journal of Developmental Psychology* **9**, 351–64.

Fein, G. G. 1981. Pretend play: an integrative review. *Cognitive Development* **52**, 1095–118.

Field, T. M., R. Woodson, R. Greenberg, D. Cohen 1982. Discrimination and imitation of facial expressions by neonates. *Science* **218**, 179–81.

Fodor, J. A. 1983. *Modularity of mind*. Cambridge, Mass.: MIT Press.

Folstein, S. & M. Rutter 1977. Infantile autism: a genetic study of 21 twin pairs. *Journal of Child Psychology and Psychiatry* **18**, 297–321.

Freeman, N. H., C. Lewis, M. J. Doherty 1991. Preschoolers' grasp of the desire for knowledge in false belief prediction: practical intelligence and verbal report. *British Journal of Developmental Psychology* **9**, 139–57.

Frith, C. D. 1992. *The cognitive neuropsychology of schizophrenia*. New Jersey: Lawrence Erlbaum.

Frith, C. D. & U. Frith 1991. Elective affinities in schizophrenia and childhood autism. In *Social psychiatry: theory, methodology and practice*, P. E. Bebbington (ed.), 65–8. New

Brunswick, NJ: Transaction.

Frith, U. 1970a. Studies in pattern detection in normal and autistic children: I. Immediate recall of auditory sequences. *Journal of Abnormal Psychology* **76**, 413–20.

Frith, U. 1970b. Studies in pattern detection in normal and autistic children: II. Reproduction and production of color sequences. *Journal of Experimental Child Psychology* **10**, 120–35.

Frith, U. 1972. Cognitive mechanisms in autism: Experiments with color and tone sequence production. *Journal of Autism and Childhood Schizophrenia* **2**, 160–73.

Frith, U. 1989a. *Autism: explaining the enigma*. Oxford: Basil Blackwell.

Frith, U. 1989b. A new look at language and communication in autism. *British Journal of Disorders of Communication* **24**, 123–50.

Frith, U. 1991a. *Autism and Asperger syndrome*. Cambridge: Cambridge University Press.

Frith, U. 1991b. Translation and annotation of 'autistic psychopathy' in childhood, by H. Asperger. See Frith (1991a), 37–92.

Frith, U. 1992. Cognitive development and cognitive deficit. *The Psychologist* **5**, 13–19.

Frith, U. & B. Hermelin 1969. The role of visual and motor cues for normal, subnormal and autistic children. *Journal of Child Psychology and Psychiatry* **10**, 153–63.

Frith, U. & M. Snowling 1983. Reading for meaning and reading for sound in autistic and dyslexic children. *Journal of Developmental Psychology* **1**, 329–42.

Frith, U., J. Morton, A. M. Leslie 1991. The cognitive basis of a biological disorder: autism. *Trends in Neuroscience* **14**, 433–8.

Frith, U., F. Happé, F. Siddons 1994. Autism and theory of mind in everyday life. *Social Development*, **3**, 108–124.

Ghaziuddin, M., L. Y. Tsai, N. Ghaziuddin 1992a. Brief report: a comparison of the diagnostic criteria for Asperger syndrome. *Journal of Autism and Developmental Disorders* **22**, 643–9.

Ghaziuddin, M., L. Y. Tsai, N. Ghaziuddin 1992b. Brief report: a reappraisal of clumsiness as a diagnostic feature of Asperger syndrome. *Journal of Autism and Developmental Disorders* **22**, 651–6.

Gillberg, C. 1986. Brief report: Onset at age 14 of a typical autistic syndrome. A case report of a girl with herpes simplex encephalitis. *Journal of Autism and Developmental Disorders* **16**, 369–75.

Gillberg, C. 1989. Asperger's syndrome in 23 Swedish children. *Developmental Medicine and Child Neurology* **31**, 520–31.

Gillberg, C. 1991. Clinical and neurobiological aspects of Asperger syndrome in six family studies. See Frith (1991a), 122–46.

Gillberg, C. 1992. The Emanuel Miller Memorial Lecture 1991: Autism and autistic-like conditions: subclasses among disorders of empathy. *Journal of Child Psychology and Psychiatry* **33**, 813–42.

Gillberg, C. & M. Coleman (eds) 1992. *The biology of the autistic syndromes – 2nd edn*. London: MacKeith.

Gillberg, C. & C. Forsell 1984. Childhood psychosis and neuro fibromatosis – more than a coincidence. *Journal of Autism and Developmental Disorders* **14**, 1–9.

Gillberg, C. & H. Schaumann 1982. Social class and infantile autism. *Journal of Autism and Developmental Disorders* **12**, 223–8.

Gillberg, C., E. Persson, M. Grufman, U. Themnér 1986. Psychiatric disorders in mildly and severely mentally retarded urban children and adolescents: epidemiological aspects. *British Journal of Psychiatry* **149**, 68–74.

Gillberg, C., S. Steffenburg, G. Jakobsson 1987. Neurobiological findings in 20 relatively gifted children with Kanner-type autism or Asperger's syndrome. *Developmental Medicine and Child Neurology* **29**, 641–9.

Gillberg, I. C. 1991. Autistic syndrome with onset at age 31 years: herpes encephalitis as a possible model for childhood autism. *Developmental Medicine and Child Neurology* **33**, 912–29.

Goodenough, D. R., F. Grandini, I. Olkin, D. Pizzamiglio, D. Thayer, H. A. Witkin 1977. A study of X chromosome linkage with field dependence and spatial visualisation. *Behaviour Genetics* **7**, 373–87.

Goodman, R. 1989. Infantile autism: a syndrome of multiple primary deficits? *Journal of Autism and Developmental Disorders* **19**, 409–24.

Goodman, R. 1990. Technical note: are perinatal complications causes or consequences of autism? *Journal of Child Psychology and Psychiatry* **31**, 809–12.

Gopnik, A. & J. Astington 1988. Children's understanding of representational change and its relation to the understanding of false belief and the appearance/reality distinction. *Child Development* **59**, 26–37.

Gottschaldt, K. 1926. Ueber den Einfluss der Erfahrung auf die Welt der Wahrnehmung von Figuren. *Psychologische Forschung* **8**, 261–317.

Grandin, T. 1984. My experiences as an autistic child and review of selected literature. *Journal of Orthomolecular Psychiatry* **13**, 144–75.

Grandin, T. & M. Scariano 1986. *Emergence labelled autistic.* Tunbridge Wells: Costello.

Green, W. H., M. Campbell, A. S. Hardesty, D. M. Grega, M. Padron-Gayor, J. Shell, L. Erlenmeyer-Kimling 1984. A comparison of schizophrenic and autistic children. *Journal of the American Academy of Child and Adolescent Psychiatry,* **23**, 399–409.

Happé, F. G. E. 1991a. The autobiographical writings of three Asperger syndrome adults: problems of interpretation and implications for theory. See Frith (1991a), 207–42.

Happé, F. G. E. 1991b. *Theory of mind and communication in autism.* PhD thesis, University of London.

Happé, F. G. E. 1993. Communicative competence and theory of mind in autism: a test of Relevance theory. *Cognition* **48**, 101–19.

Happé, F. G. E. 1994a. An advanced test of theory of mind: understanding of story characters' thoughts and feelings by able autistic, mentally handicapped and normal children and adults. *Journal of Autism and Developmental Disorders* **24**, 129–54.

Happé, F. G. E. 1994b. Annotation: psychological theories of autism: the 'theory of mind' account and rival theories. *Journal of Child Psychology and Psychiatry* **35**, 215–29.

Happé, F. G. E. 1994c. The role of age and verbal ability in the theory of mind task performance of subjects with autism. *Child Development,* in press.

Happé, F. G. E. 1994d. Central coherence, Block Design errors, and global–local similarity judgement in autistic subjects. In preparation.

Happé, F. G. E. 1994e. Wechsler IQ profile and theory of mind in autism: a research note. *Journal of Child Psychology and Psychiatry,* in press.

Happé, F. & U. Frith 1994. Theory of mind in autism. In *Learning and Cognition in Autism*, E. Schopler & G. B. Mesibov (eds), in press. New York: Plenum Press.

Harris, P. L. 1993. Pretending and planning. See Baron-Cohen et al. (1993b), 228–46.

Hart, C. 1989. *Without reason: a family copes with two generations of autism.* New York: Penguin Books.

Hermelin, B. & N. O'Connor 1967. Remembering of words by psychotic and subnormal children. *British Journal of Psychology* **58**, 213–8.

Hermelin, B. & N. O'Connor 1970. *Psychological experiments with autistic children.* Oxford: Pergamon Press.

Hermelin, B. & N. O'Connor 1986. Idiot savant calendrical calculators: rules and regularities. *Psychological Medicine* **16**, 885–93.

Hertzig, M. E., M. E. Snow, M. Sherman 1989. Affect and cognition in autism. *Journal of the American Academy of Child and Adolescent Psychiatry,* **28**, 195–9.

Hobson, R. P. 1986a. The autistic child's appraisal of expressions of emotion. *Journal of Child Psychology and Psychiatry* **27**, 321–42.

Hobson, R. P. 1986b. The autistic child's appraisal of expressions of emotion: a further study. *Journal of Child Psychology and Psychiatry* **27**, 671–80.

Hobson, R. P. 1989. Beyond cognition: a theory of autism. In *Autism: nature, diagnosis and treatment*, G. Dawson (ed.), 22–48. New York: Guildford Press.

Hobson, R. P. 1990. On acquiring knowledge about people, and the capacity to pretend: a response to Leslie. *Psychological Review* **97**, 114–21.

Hobson, R. P. 1993a. *Autism and the development of mind.* Hove, East Sussex: Lawrence Erlbaum Associates.

Hobson, R. P. 1993b. Understanding persons: the role of affect. See Baron-Cohen et al. (1993b) 204–27.

Hobson, R. P., J. Ouston, T. Lee 1988. What's in a face? The case of autism. *British Journal of Psychology* **79**, 441–53.

Hobson, R. P., J. Ouston, T. Lee 1989. Naming emotion in faces and voices: abilities and disabilities in autism and mental retardation. *British Journal of Developmental Psychology* **7**, 237–50.

Hornik, R., N. Risenhoover, M. Gunnar 1987. The effect of maternal positive, neutral, and negative affective communications on infant responses to new toys. *Child Development* **58**, 937–44.

Howlin, P. & M. Rutter 1987. *The treatment of autistic children.* Chichester: John Wiley.

Hughes, C. H. 1993. *Executive dysfunction in autism.* Doctoral thesis, University of Cambridge.

Hughes, C. H. & J. Russell 1993. Autistic children's difficulty with mental disengagement from an object: its implications for theories of autism. *Developmental Psychology* **29**, 498–510.

Hunt, A. & J. Dennis 1987. Psychiatric disorder among children with tuberous sclerosis. *Developmental Medicine and Child Neurology* **29**, 190–8.

Hurlburt, R. T. 1990. *Sampling normal and schizophrenic inner experience.* New York: Plenum Press.

Hurlburt, R., F. Happé, U. Frith 1994. Sampling the inner experience of autism: a preliminary report. *Psychological Medicine* **24**.

Johnson, D. J. & H. R. Myklebust 1971. *Learning disabilities*. New York: Grune & Stratton.

Johnson, M. H., F. Siddons, U. Frith, J. Morton 1992. Can autism be predicted on the basis of infant screening tests? *Developmental Medicine and Child Neurology* **34**, 316–20.

Kang, K. S. & D. K. Kang (eds) 1988. *Folktales of India*. London: Asia Publishing House.

Kanner, L. 1943. Autistic disturbances of affective contact. *Nervous Child* **2**, 217–50.

Kanner, L. 1973. *Childhood psychosis: initial studies and new insights*. Washington, DC: V. H. Winston.

Kanner, L. & L. Eisenberg 1956. Early infantile autism 1943–1955. *American Journal of Orthopsychiatry* **26**, 55–65.

Kay, P. & I. Kolvin 1987. Childhood psychoses and their borderlands. *British Medical Bulletin* **43**, 570–86.

Kimchi, R. & S. E. Palmer 1982. Form and texture in hierarchically constructed patterns. *Journal of Experimental Psychology: Human Perception and Performance* **8**, 521–35.

Klin, A., F. R. Volkmar, S. S. Sparrow 1992. Autistic social dysfunction: some limitations of the theory of mind hypothesis. *Journal of Child Psychology and Psychiatry* **33**, 861–76.

Knobloch, H. & B. Pasamanick 1975. Some etiologic and prognostic factors in early infantile autism and psychosis. *Pediatrics* **55**, 182–91.

Koffka, K. 1935. *Principles of Gestalt psychology*. New York: Harcourt Brace.

Kohs, S. C. 1923. *Intelligence measurement*. New York: MacMillan.

Kramer, J. H., E. Kaplan, M. J. Blusewicz, K. A. Preston 1991. Visual hierarchical analysis of block design configural errors. *Journal of Clinical and Experimental Neuropsychology* **13**, 455–65.

Landa, R., S. E. Folstein, C. Isaacs 1991. Spontaneous narrative-discourse performance of parents of autistic individuals. *Journal of Speech and Hearing Research* **34**, 1339–45.

Langdell, T. 1978. Recognition of faces: an approach to the study of autism. *Journal of Child Psychology and Psychiatry* **19**, 255–68.

Leekam, S. & J. Perner 1991. Does the autistic child have a metarepresentational deficit? *Cognition* **40**, 203–18.

Leiner, H. C., A. L. Leiner, R. S. Dow 1986. Does the cerebellum contribute to mental skills? *Behavioral Neuroscience* **100**, 443–54.

Leslie, A. M. 1987. Pretence and representation: The origins of "theory of mind". *Psychological Review* **94**, 412–26.

Leslie, A. M. 1988. Some implications of pretence for mechanisms underlying the child's theory of mind. In *Developing theories of mind*, J. W. Astington, P. L. Harris, D. R. Olson (eds), 19–46. New York: Cambridge University Press.

Leslie, A. M. & U. Frith 1988. Autistic children's understanding of seeing, knowing and believing. *British Journal of Developmental Psychology* **6**, 315–24.

Leslie A. M. & F. Happé 1989. Autism and ostensive communication: the relevance of metarepresentation. *Development and Psychopathology* **1**, 205–12.

Leslie, A. M. & D. Roth 1993. What autism teaches us about metarepresentation. See Baron-Cohen et al. (1993b), 83–111.

Leslie, A. M. & L. Thaiss 1992. Domain specificity in conceptual development: evidence from autism. *Cognition* **43**, 225–51.

Lister, S. 1992. *The early detection of social and communication impairments*. Doctoral thesis,

University of London.

Lockyer, L. & M. Rutter 1970. A five to fifteen year follow-up study of infantile psychosis: IV. Patterns of cognitive ability. *British Journal of Social and Clinical Psychology* **9**, 152–63.

Lord, C. 1991. Follow-up of two-year-olds referred for possible autism. Paper presented at the Biennial Meeting of the Society for Research in Child Development, Seattle.

Lord, C. & E. Schopler 1987. Neurobiological implications of sex differences in autism. In *Neurobiological issues in autism*, E. Schopler & G. Mesibov (eds), 192–211. New York: Plenum Press.

Lotter, V. 1966. Epidemiology of autistic conditions in young children: I. Prevalence. *Social Psychiatry* **1**, 124–37.

Lotter, V. 1974. Factors related to outcome in autistic children. *Journal of Autism and Childhood Schizophrenia* **4**, 263–77.

Lovaas, O. I., L. Schreibman, R. Koegel, R. Rehm 1971. Selective responding by autistic children to multiple sensory input. *Journal of Abnormal Psychology* **77**, 211–22.

Macdonald, H., M. Rutter, P. Howlin, P. Rios, A. Le Couteur, C. Evered, S. Folstein 1989. Recognition and expression of emotional cues by autistic and normal adults. *Journal of Child Psychology and Psychiatry* **30**, 865–77.

McDonnell, J. T. 1993. *News from the border: a mother's memoir of her autistic son*. New York: Ticknor & Fields.

Meltzoff, A. N. 1988. Infant imitation and memory: nine-month-olds in immediate and differed tests. *Child Development* **59**, 217–25.

Meltzoff, A. N. & A. Gopnik 1993. The role of imitation in understanding persons and developing a theory of mind. See Baron-Cohen et al. (1993b), 335–66.

Meltzoff, A. N. & M. K. Moore 1977. Imitation of facial and manual gestures by human neonates. *Science* **198**, 75–8.

Miedzianik, D. C. 1986. *My autobiography*. Nottingham: University of Nottingham.

Mitchell, P. & H. Lacohée 1991. Children's early understanding of false belief. *Cognition* **39**, 107–27.

Morton, J. & U. Frith 1994. Causal modelling: a structural approach to developmental psychopathology. In *Manual of developmental psychopathology*, vol. 1, D. Cicchetti & D. J. Cohen (eds), ch. 13, in press. New York: John Wiley.

Mottron, L. & S. Belleville 1993. A study of perceptual analysis in a high-level autistic subject with exceptional graphic abilities. *Brain and Cognition* **23**, 279–309.

Mundy, P. & M. Sigman 1989. The theoretical implications of joint attention deficits in autism. *Development and Psychopathology* **1**, 173–83.

Mundy, P., M. Sigman, C. Kasari 1993. Theory of mind and joint attention deficits in autism. See Baron-Cohen et al. (1993b), 181–204.

Nagy, J. & P. Szatmari 1986. A chart review of schizotypal personality disorders in children. *Journal of Autism and Developmental Disorders* **16**, 351–67.

Navon, D. 1977. Forest before trees: the precedence of global features in visual perception. *Cognitive Psychology* **9**, 353–83.

Newson, E., M. Dawson, P. Everard 1984a. The natural history of able autistic people: their management and functioning in social context. Summary of the report to DHSS in four parts. *Communication* **18**, 1–4.

Newson, E., M. Dawson, P. Everard 1984b. The natural history of able autistic people: their management and functioning in social context. Summary of the report to the DHSS in four parts. *Communication* **19,** 1–2.

Norris, D. 1990. How to build a connectionist idiot savant. *Cognition* **35**, 277–91.

Olsson, I., S. Steffenburg, C. Gillberg 1988. Epilepsy in autism and autistic–like conditions – a population based study. *Archives of Neurology* **45**, 666–8.

Ozonoff, S., B. F. Pennington, S. J. Rogers 1990. Are there emotion perception deficits in young autistic children? *Journal of Child Psychology and Psychiatry* **51**, 343–61.

Ozonoff, S., B. F. Pennington, S. J. Rogers 1991a. Executive function deficits in high-functioning autistic children: relationship to theory of mind. *Journal of Child Psychology and Psychiatry* **32**, 1081–106.

Ozonoff, S., S. J. Rogers, B. F. Pennington 1991b. Asperger's syndrome: evidence of an empirical distinction from high-functioning autism. *Journal of Child Psychology and Psychiatry* **32**, 1107–22.

Palmer, S. E. 1975. The effects of contextual scenes on the identification of objects. *Memory and Cognition* **3**, 519–26.

Panksepp, J. & T. L. Sahley 1987. Possible brain opiod involvement in disrupted social intent and language development of autism. In *Neurobiological issues in autism*, E. Schopler & G.B. Mesibov (eds), 357–72. New York: Plenum Press.

Park, C. C. 1987. *The siege: the first eight years of an autistic child*; second edn with epilogue: Fifteen years and after. Boston, Mass.: Atlantic-Little, Brown.

Paul, R. 1987. Communication. In *Handbook of autism and pervasive developmental disorders*, D. J. Cohen, A. M. Donnellan, R. Paul (eds), 61–84. New York: John Wiley.

Pennington, B. F. & M. Welsh 1994. Neuropsychology and developmental psychopathology. In *Manual of developmental psychopathology*, vol. 1, D. Cicchetti & D. J. Cohen (eds), in press. New York: Plenum Press.

Perner, J. 1993. The theory of mind deficit in autism: rethinking the metarepresentation theory. See Baron-Cohen et al. (1993b), 112–37.

Perner, J. & H. Wimmer 1985. "John *thinks* that Mary thinks that . . . " Attribution of second-order beliefs by 5–10 year old children. *Journal of Experimental Child Psychology* **39**, 437–71.

Perner, J., U. Frith, A. M. Leslie, S. R. Leekam 1989. Exploration of the autistic child's theory of mind: knowledge, belief, and communication. *Child Development* **60**, 689–700.

Petty, L., E. M. Ornitz, J. D. Michelman, E. G. Zimmerman 1984. Autistic children who become schizophrenic. *Archives of General Psychiatry* **41**, 129–35.

Phillips, W. 1993. *Understanding intention and desire by children with autism*. PhD thesis, University of London.

Phillips, W., S. Baron-Cohen, M. Rutter 1992. The role of eye contact in goal detection: evidence from normal infants and children with autism or mental handicap. *Development and Psychopathology* **4**, 375–83.

Pratt, C. & P. E. Bryant 1990. Young children understand that looking leads to knowing (so long as they are looking into a single barrel). *Child Development* **61**, 973–82.

Premack, D. & G. Woodruff 1978. Does the chimpanzee have a theory of mind? *Behavioural and Brain Sciences* **4**, 515–26.

Prior, M. R. 1979. Cognitive abilities and disabilities in infantile autism: a review. *Journal of Abnormal Child Psychology* **7**, 357–80.

Prior, M. & W. Hoffman 1990. Brief report: neuropsychological testing of autistic children through an exploration with frontal lobe tests. *Journal of Autism and Developmental Disorders* **20**, 581–90.

Prior, M. R., B. Dahlstrom, T. L. Squires 1990. Autistic children's knowledge of thinking and feeling states in other people. *Journal of Child Psychology and Psychiatry* **31**, 587–601.

Rapin, I. & D. Allen 1983. Developmental language disorders: nosological considerations. In *Neuropsychology of language, reading and spelling*, U. Kirk (ed.), 155–84. New York: Academic Press.

Reed, T. & C. Peterson 1990. A comparative study of autistic subjects' performance at two levels of visual and cognitive perspective taking. *Journal of Autism and Developmental Disorders* **20**, 555–68.

Reiss, A. L., C. Feinstein & I. C. Rosenbaum 1986. Autism and genetic disorders. *Schizophrenia Bulletin* **12**, 724–38.

Rhodes, G., S. Brake, A. P. Atkinson 1993. What's lost in inverted faces? *Cognition* **47**, 25–57.

Rimland, B. 1978. Savant capabilities of autistic children and their cognitive implications. In *Cognitive defects in the development of mental illness*, G. Serban (ed.), 43–65. New York: Bruner/Mazel.

Rimland, B. & A. L. Hill 1984. Idiot savants. In *Mental retardation and developmental disabilities*, vol. 13, Wortis, J. (ed.), 155–69. New York: Plenum Press.

Ritvo, E. R., B. J. Freeman, A. B. Scheibel, T. Duong, H. Robinson, D. Guthrie, A. Ritvo 1986. Lower Purkinje cell counts in the cerebella of four autistic subjects: initial findings of the UCLA-NSAC autopsy research report. *American Journal of Psychiatry* **143**, 862–6.

Robinson, J. F. & L. J. Vitale 1954. Children with circumscribed interest patterns. *American Journal of Orthopsychiatry* **24**, 755–66.

Rogers, S. J. & B. F. Pennington 1991. A theoretical approach to the deficits in infantile autism. *Development and Psychopathology* **3**, 137–62.

Rogers, S. J. & C. B. Pulchalski 1984. Development of symbolic play in visually impaired infants. *Papers in Early Childhood Special Education* **3**, 57–64.

Roth, D. & A. M. Leslie 1991. The recognition of attitude conveyed by utterances: a study of preschool and autistic children. *British Journal of Developmental Psychology* **9**, 315–30.

Rumsey, J. M. & S. D. Hamburger 1988. Neuropsychological findings in high-functioning men with infantile autism, residual state. *Journal of Clinical and Experimental Neuropsychology* **10**, 201–21.

Russell, J., N. Mauthner, S. Sharpe, T. Tidswell 1991. The "windows" task as a measure of strategic deception in preschoolers and autistic subjects. *British Journal of Developmental Psychology* **9**, 331–49.

Rutter, M. 1978. Diagnosis and definition of childhood autism. *Journal of Autism and Childhood Schizophrenia* **8**, 139–61.

Rutter, M. & E. Schopler 1987. Autism and pervasive developmental disorders: conceptual and diagnostic issues. *Journal of Autism and Developmetal Disorders* **17**, 159–86.

Rutter, M., H. Macdonald, A. LeCouteur, R. Harrington, P. Bolton, A. Bailey 1990. Genetic factors in child psychiatric disorders: II. Empirical findings. *Journal of Child Psychology and Psychiatry* **31**, 39–83.

Schopler, E. 1985. Convergence of learning disability, higher-level autism and Asperger's syndrome. *Journal of Autism and Developmental Disorders* **15**, 359.

Schopler, E. & G. B. Mesibov (eds) 1983. *Autism in adolescents and adults*. In *Current issues in autism* [series]. New York: Plenum Press.

Schopler, E. & G. B. Mesibov (eds) 1985. *Communication problems in autism*. In *Current issues in autism* [series]. New York: Plenum Press.

Schopler, E. & G. B. Mesibov (eds) 1987. *Neurobiological issues in autism*. In *Current issues in autism* [series]. New York: Plenum Press.

Schopler, E., R. J. Reichler, R. F. DeVellis, K. Daly 1980. Towards objective classification of childhood autism: Childhood Autism Rating Scale (CARS). *Journal of Autism and Developmental Disorders* **10**, 91–103.

Schreibman, L. 1988. *Autism*. London: Sage.

Selfe, L. 1977. *Nadia: A case of extraordinary drawing ability in an autistic child*. London: Academic Press.

Semrud-Clikeman, M. & G. W. Hynd 1990. Right hemisphere dysfunction in nonverbal learning disabilities: Social, academic and adaptive functioning in adults and children. *Psychological Bulletin* **107**, 196–209.

Shah, A. 1988. *Visuo-spatial islets of abilities and intellectual functioning in autism*. PhD thesis, University of London.

Shah, A. & U. Frith 1983. An islet of ability in autistic children: a research note. *Journal of Child Psychology and Psychiatry* **24**, 613–20.

Shah, A. & U. Frith 1993. Why do autistic individuals show superior performance on the Block Design task? *Journal of Child Psychology and Psychiatry* **34**, 1351–64.

Shah, A., N. Holmes, L. Wing 1982. Prevalence of autism and related conditions in adults in a mental handicap hospital. *Applied Research in Mental Handicap* **3**, 303–17.

Shallice, T. & P. Burgess 1991. Deficits in strategy application following frontal lobe damage in man. *Brain* **114**, 727–41.

Shapiro, T. D., M. Sherman, G. Calamari, D. Koch 1987. Attachment in autism and other developmental disorders. *Journal of the Academy of Child and Adolescent Psychiatry* **26**, 480–84.

Shatz, M., H. M. Wellman, S. Silber 1983. The acquisition of mental verbs: a systematic investigation of first references to mental state. *Cognition* **14**, 301–21.

Siegal, M. & K. Beattie 1991. Where to look first for children's knowledge of false beliefs. *Cognition* **38**, 1–12.

Siegel, B., T. F. Anders, R. D. Ciaranello, B. Bienenstock, H. C. Kraemer 1986. Empirically derived subclassification of the autistic syndrome. *Journal of Autism and Developmental Disorders* **16**, 275–93.

Sigman, M. & P. Mundy 1989. Social attachments in autistic children. *Journal of the American Academy of Child and Adolescent Psychiatry* **28**, 74–81.

Sigman, M. & J. A. Ungerer 1984. Attachment behaviours in autistic children. *Journal of Autism and Developmental Disorders* **14**, 231–44.

Sigman, M., P. Mundy, T. Sherman, J. Ungerer 1986. Social interactions of autistic, mentally retarded, and normal children and their caregivers. *Journal of Child Psychology and Psychiatry* **27**, 647–56.

Sigman, M., C. Kasari, J. Kwon, N. Yirmiya 1992. Responses to the negative emotions of others by autistic, mentally retarded, and normal children. *Child Development* **63**, 796–807.

Smalley, S. L. & R. F. Asarnow 1990. Brief report: cognitive subclinical markers in autism. *Journal of Autism and Developmental Disorders* **20**, 271–8.

Smalley, S. L., R. F. Asarnow, A. Spence 1988. Autism and genetics: a decade of research. *Archives of General Psychiatry* **45**, 953–61.

Smith, U. (ed.) 1979. *Folktales from Australia's children of the world*. Sydney: Paul Hamlyn.

Snowling, M. 1987. *Dyslexia: a cognitive developmental perspective*. Oxford: Basil Blackwell.

Snowling, M. & U. Frith 1986. Comprehension in 'hyperlexic' readers. *Journal of Experimental Child Psychology* **42**, 392–415.

Sodian, B. & U. Frith 1992. Deception and sabotage in autistic, retarded and normal children. *Journal of Child Psychology and Psychiatry* **33**, 591–605.

Sparling, J. W. 1991. Brief report: a prospective case report of infantile autism from pregnancy to four years. *Journal of Autism and Developmental Disorders* **21**, 229–36

Sparrow, S., D. Balla, D. Cichetti 1984. *Vineland Adaptive Behaviour Scales (survey form)*. Circle Pines, Minn.: American Guidance Services.

Sperber, D. & D. Wilson 1986. *Relevance: communication and cognition*. Oxford: Basil Blackwell.

Steffenburg, S. 1991. Neuropsychiatric assessment of children with autism: a population-based study. *Developmental Medicine and Child Neurology* **33**, 495–511.

Steffenburg, S. & C. Gillberg 1986. Autism and autistic-like conditions in Swedish rural and urban areas: a population study. *British Journal of Psychiatry* **149**, 81–7.

Steffenburg, S. & C. Gillberg 1989. The etiology of autism. In *Diagnosis and treatment of autism*, C. Gillberg (ed.), 63–82. New York: Plenum Press.

Szatmari, P. & M. B. Jones 1991. IQ and the genetics of autism. *Journal of Child Psychology and Psychiatry* **32**, 897–908.

Szatmari, P., G. Bartolucci, A. Finlayson, L. Krames 1986. A vote for Asperger's syndrome. *Journal of Autism and Developmental Disorders* **16**, 515–17.

Szatmari, P., R. Bremner, J. Nagy 1989a. Asperger's syndrome: a review of clinical features. *Canadian Journal of Psychiatry* **34**, 554–60.

Szatmari, P., G. Bartolucci, R. Bremner 1989b. Asperger's syndrome and autism: comparisons on early history and outcome. *Developmental Medicine and Child Neurology* **31**, 709–20.

Szatmari, P., G. Bartolucci, R. Bremner, S. Bond, S. Rich 1989c. A follow-up study of high-functioning autistic children. *Journal of Autism and Developmental Disorders* **19**, 213–25.

Szatmari, P., L. Tuff, M. A. J. Finlayson, G. Bartolucci 1990. Asperger's syndrome and autism: neurocognitive aspects. *Journal of the American Academy of Child and Adolescent Psychiatry*, **29**, 130–6.

Tager-Flusberg, H. 1981. On the nature of linguistic functioning in early infantile autism. *Journal of Autism and Developmental Disorders* **11**, 45–56.

Tager-Flusberg, H. 1991. Semantic processing in the free recall of autistic children:

143

further evidence for a cognitive deficit. *British Journal of Developmental Psychology* **9**, 417–30.

Tager-Flusberg, H. 1993. What language reveals about the understanding of minds in children with autism. See Baron-Cohen et al. (1993b), 138–57.

Tanaka, J. W. & M. J. Farah 1993. Parts and wholes in face recognition. *Quarterly Journal of Experimental Psychology* **46A**, 225–45.

Tanoue, Y., S. Oda, F. Asano, K. Kawashima 1988. Epidemiology of infantile autism in southern Ibaraki, Japan: differences in prevalence rates in birth cohorts. *Journal of Autism and Developmental Disorders* **18**, 155–66.

Tantam, D. J. H. 1988a. Lifelong eccentricity and social isolation: I. Psychiatric, social and forensic aspects. *British Journal of Psychiatry* **153**, 777–82.

Tantam, D. J. H. 1988b. Lifelong eccentricity and social isolation: II. Asperger's syndrome or schizoid personality disorder? *British Journal of Psychiatry* **153**, 783–91.

Tantam, D. J. H. 1988c. Asperger's syndrome. An annotation. *Journal of Child Psychology and Psychiatry* **29**, 245–55.

Tantam, D. J. H. 1991. Asperger's syndrome in adulthood. See Frith (1991a), 147–83.

Trabasso, T. & S. Suh 1993. Understanding text: achieving explanatory coherence through on-line inferences and mental operations in working memory. *Discourse Processes* **16**, 3–34.

Van Krevelen, D. 1971. Early infantile autism and autistic psychopathy. *Journal of Autism and Childhood Schizophrenia* **1**, 82–6.

Voeller, K. K. S. 1986. Right hemisphere deficit syndrome in children. *American Journal of Psychiatry* **143**, 1004–9.

Volkmar, F. R., C. Paul, D. J. Cohen 1985. The use of "Asperger's syndrome". *Journal of Autism and Developmental Disorders* **15**, 437–9.

Volkmar, F. R., D. J. Cohen, J. D. Bregman, M. Y. Hooks, J. M. Stevenson 1989. An examination of social typologies in autism. *Journal of the American Academy of Child and Adolescent Psychiatry*, **28**, 82–6.

Walker, A. S. 1982. Intermodal perception of expressive behaviours by human infants. *Journal of Experimental Child Psychology* **33**, 514–35.

Watkin, J. M., R. F. Asarnow, P. E. Tanguay 1988. Symptom development in childhood onset schizophrenia. *Journal of Child Psychology and Psychiatry* **29**, 865–78.

Wechsler, D. 1974. *Wechsler Intelligence Scale for Children – Revised*. New York: The Psychological Corporation.

Wechsler, D. 1981. *Wechsler Adult Intelligence Scales – Revised*. New York: The Psychological Corporation.

Weeks, S. J. & R. P. Hobson 1987. The salience of facial expression for autistic children. *Journal of Child Psychology and Psychiatry* **28**, 137–52.

Weintraub, S. & M. M. Mesulam 1983. Developmental learning disabilities of the right hemisphere. Emotional, interpersonal and cognitive components. *Archives of Neurology* **40**, 463–5.

Wellman, H. M. & D. Estes 1986. Early understanding of mental entities: a re-examination of childhood realism. *Child Development* **57**, 910–23.

Wetherby, A. M. & C. A. Prutting 1984. Profiles of communicative and cognitive-social abilities in autistic children. *Journal of Speech and Hearing Research* **27**, 364–77.

Whiten, A. (ed.). 1991. *Natural theories of mind: evolution, development and simulation of every-day mindreading.* Oxford: Basil Blackwell.

Williams, D. 1992. *Nobody nowhere.* London: Doubleday.

Wimmer, H. & J. Perner 1983. Beliefs about beliefs: representation and the constraining function of wrong beliefs in young children's understanding of deception. *Cognition* **13**, 103–28.

Wing, L. 1971. *Autistic children: a guide for parents.* London: Constable.

Wing, L. 1976. Diagnosis, clinical description and prognosis. In *Early childhood autism*, 2nd edn, L. Wing (ed.), 15–64. Oxford: Pergamon Press.

Wing, L. 1980. Childhood autism and social class: a question of selection. *British Journal of Psychiatry* **137**, 410–17.

Wing, L. 1981a. Asperger's syndrome: a clinical account. *Psychological Medicine* **11**, 115–29.

Wing, L. 1981b. Language, social, and cognitive impairments in autism and severe mental retardation. *Journal of Autism and Developmental Disorders* **11**, 31–44.

Wing, L. 1984. Letter: schizoid personality in childhood. *British Journal of Psychiatry* **145**, 444.

Wing, L. 1988. The continuum of autistic characteristics. In *Diagnosis and assessment in autism*, E. Schopler & G. B. Mesibov (eds), 91–110. New York: Plenum Press.

Wing, L. & A. J. Attwood 1987. Syndromes of autism and atypical development. In *Handbook of autism and pervasive developmental disorders*, D. J. Cohen, A. Donnellan, R. Paul (eds), 3–19. New York: John Wiley.

Wing, L. & J. Gould 1978. Systematic recording of behaviours and skills of retarded and psychotic children. *Journal of Autism and Childhood Schizophrenia* **8**, 79–97.

Wing, L. & J. Gould 1979. Severe impairments of social interaction and associated abnormalities in children: epidemiology and classification. *Journal of Autism and Developmental Disorders* **9**, 11–29.

Wing, L. & J. K. Wing 1971. Multiple impairments in early childhood autism. *Journal of Autism and Childhood Schizophrenia* **1**, 256–66.

Wing, L., J. Gould, S. R. Yeates, L. M. Brierley 1977. Symbolic play in severely mentally retarded and autistic children. *Journal of Child Psychology and Psychiatry* **18**, 167–78.

Witkin, H. A., P. K. Oltman, E. Raskin, S. Karp 1971. *A manual for the Embedded Figures Test.* California: Consulting Psychologists Press.

Wolff, S. & A. Barlow 1979. Schizoid personality in childhood: a comparative study of schizoid, autistic and normal children. *British Journal of Psychology and Psychiatry* **20**, 29–46.

Wolff, S. & S. Chess 1964. A behavioural study of schizophrenic children. *Acta Psychiatrica Scandinavica* **40**, 438–66.

Wolff, S. & J. Chick 1980. Schizoid personality in childhood: a controlled follow-up study. *Psychological Medicine* **10**, 85–100.

Wolff, S. & A. Cull 1986. 'Schizoid' personality and antisocial conduct: a retrospective case note study. *Psychological Medicine* **16**, 677–87.

World Health Organization 1990. *International classification of diseases:*, 10th revision,. Ch. V. Mental and behavioural disorders (including disorders of psychological development). Diagnostic criteria for research. (May 1990 draft for field trials.) Geneva: WHO [unpublished].

Wulff, S. B. 1985. The symbolic and object play of children with autism: a review. *Journal of Autism and Developmental Disorders* **15**, 139–48.

Yirmiya, N., M. D. Sigman, C. Kasari, P. Mundy 1992. Empathy and cognition in high-functioning children with autism. *Child Development* **63**, 150–60.

Zaitchik, D. 1990. When representations conflict with reality: the preschoolers' problem with false belief and "false" photographs. *Cognition* **35**, 41–68.

Subject index

Author index

Forsell, C.   30
Freeman, N. H.   44
Frith, C. D.   99
Frith, U.   vii, 2, 7, 11, 12, 14, 17, 36, 41,
    42, 43, 49, 51, 52, 54, 55, 56, 59, 68, 71,
    73, 74, 75, 76, 82, 92, 99, 101, 114, 116,
    117, 119, 120, 121, 123, 124, 127

Ghaziuddin, M.   91, 96, 101
Gillberg, C.   25, 26, 28, 29, 30, 33, 85,
    90, 91, 96, 97
Gittens, T.   vii
Goodenough, D. R.   125
Goodman, R.   29, 52
Gopnik, A.   45, 64, 68
Gottschaldt, K.   119
Grandin, T.   vii
Green, W. H.   29

Hamburger, S. D.   31, 97
Happé, F. G. E.   51, 59, 60, 62, 71, 72,
    73, 76, 77, 79, 82, 113, 114, 122, 123,
    124
Harris, P. L.   45, 55
Hart, C.   vii, 115
Hermelin, B.   115–17, 126
Hill, A. L.   19
Hobson, R. P.   vii, 36, 61, 62, 66, 116,
    120, 127
Hoffman, W.   31
Hornik, R.   36
Howlin, P.   vii
Hughes, C. H.   54, 55
Hunt, A.   30
Hurlburt, R. T.   48
Hynd, G. W.   106, 112
Johnson, D. J.   106
Johnson, M. H.   21
Jones, M. B.   25, 30, 89

Kang, K. S.   8
Kanner, L.   7, 9–15, 18–20, 25, 27, 83–4,
    87, 91–2, 96, 99–100, 102, 104, 106,
    108, 115, 119, 120, 127
Kay, P.   107
Kemper, T. L.   31
Kerbeshian, J.   84, 85, 93

Kimchi, R.   121
Klin, A.   63
Koffka, K.   119
Kohs, S. C.   119
Kolvin, I.   107
Kramer, J. H.   121

Lacohée, H.   44
Landa, R.   125
Langdell, T.   62, 116, 120
Leekam, S.   48, 55, 71, 114
Leiner, H. C.   31
Leslie, A. M.   38–40, 45–6, 48, 51, 55,
    62, 71, 73, 114, 125
Lewy, A.   52
Lister, S.   21
Lockyer, L.   19, 97, 119
Lord, C.   25, 29, 65
Lotter, V.   25, 29
Lovaas, O. I.   16

Macdonald, H.   36
Mamelle, N.   25
Maurer, R. G.   52
McDonnell, J. T.   vii, 115
McKissick, F. C.   35
Meltzoff, A. N.   35, 64
Mesibov, G. B.   vii, 26, 28, 30, 33, 36, 51,
    82
Mesulam, M. M.   106
Miedzianik, D. C.   vii
Mitchell, P.   44
Moore, M. K.   35
Morton, J.   2, 51, 52
Mottron, L.   123
Mundy, P.   35, 62
Myklebust, H. R.   106

Nagy, J.   108
Navon, D.   126
Newson, E.   97
Norris, D.   126

O'Connor, N.   115–17, 126
Olsson, I.   28
Ozonoff, S.   31, 35, 36, 52, 55, 59–61,
    70, 85, 95, 99, 100

151